Chapter One:

SIX MILLION JEWS MURDERED!! September 1, 1939 World War II began. In Europe, the Jewish population was over nine million Jews. The Nazi's main goal was to extinguish all of the Jews in Europe. They did not only kill the Jews – they killed Gypsies, the disabled such as those who were mentally and physically challenged, Communists, Socialists, Jehovah's Witnesses, and Homosexuals. Anyone who was not a Pure Aryan German was either killed or placed in concentration camps. 48,231,700 lives were lost between 1939 and 1945 in World War II.

The Nazis believed that anyone different from them deserved to be exterminated such as Gypsies who are free spirited and nomadic people. Another religion the Nazis persecuted, besides the Jewish religion were the Jehovah's Witnesses. According to the free dictionary and the United States Holocaust Memorial Museum, "A Jehovah's Witness is a person who is a member of a Christian Church of American origin, the followers of which believe that the end of the present world system of government is near, that all other Churches and religions are false or evil, that all war is unlawful, and that the civil law must be resisted whenever it conflicts with their Church's own religious principles."

Political people whose views did not conform to the Nazi party were also exterminated. Communists are people that believe in class war, that property should be publicly owned, and every person should work and be paid according to their abilities and needs. Socialists are people that believe in a political and economic theory that everything that happens such as production, exchange, and the whole community should own everything that is worked for as a group. All of these people were killed because they did not believe in what the Germans believed in.

A man named Adolf Hitler was the man behind the cause of this mass extermination. Europe was in a state of depression; quite severe and the citizens believed anything anyone said that would help them escape their financial crisis. Hitler was a great speaker and he was able to persuade many people that the Jewish people were the main reason why Europe was in poverty. His speeches convinced the people to help him with his "amazing" plan. Hitler was an evil man; he destroyed families and communities, he tortured people in ways unimaginable and massacred millions of innocent lives in the most horrible and atrocious ways.

Pure Aryan Germans, according to schoolhistory.co.uk, "The Aryan race is tall, long legged, and slim. The race is narrow-faced, with a narrow forehead, a narrow high built nose and a lower jaw and prominent chin, the skin is rosy bright and the blood shines through, the hair is smooth, straight or wavy - possibly curly in childhood. The color is blond." Also to be a Pure Aryan German, a person must come from a clean line of German parents, grandparents, etc. Adolf Hitler believed that the Germans lost the First World War because the German race was too weak. He believed that since Pure Aryans were marrying non-Aryans, the German race was becoming weaker. Hitler said that the way they could win World War II was to become a very strong race by only marrying Pure Aryans. He wanted Germans to become the master race. The way this was encouraged was that he had people place propaganda posters all around Europe about Pure Aryan Germans. Hitler himself was not a Pure Aryan. He did not have blond hair or blue eyes, which a Pure Aryan should have; he actually had black hair and brown eyes.

Horrific violence occurred the night of "Kristallnacht". Kristallnacht means "Night of Broken Glass." A wave of anti-Jewish riots took place on November 9 and 10, 1938. The cause of "Kristallnacht" was blamed on the shooting death of a German embassy official by a German Jew of Polish ancestry. But in truth, it was a failed gay romance between the two men. The Germans did not want the public to find out that a Nazi was a homosexual, so they covered the story up by blaming the entire "Kristallnacht" riot on the fact that a Jew killed a Nazi. This happened throughout Germany and was a shocking event that no one will ever forget. Shards of glass lined the German streets from the windows of Jewish owned businesses, homes, and synagogues. Dragged brutally from their homes, many Jews were murdered and tortured on the night of "Kristallnacht". They were forced to clean the streets on their hands and knees with their own toothbrushes. The religious Jews were ridiculed while their beards were cut off for public humiliation. Synagogues, Torahs and any religious artifacts were burned throughout the towns all over Germany. After these two horrific days, the Germans blamed the mess on the Jewish people and said that the Jews had to pay for all of the damages and clean up the mess that they created. The German government fined the Jews one billion Reichsmarks (the German currency) for the damage. The Jews also had to pay another hundred million Reichsmarks to clear the wreckage. Kristallnacht marked the beginning of the end for the Jewish people.

In October 1939, the Nazis began to establish Ghettos throughout Europe to segregate the Jewish population from the remainder of the non-Jewish population. The first ghetto was created in Poland in the town of Piotrków Trybunalski. All Jews were forced to leave their homes and move into the Ghetto. A ghetto is usually found in a poor area of town where the Jewish population were forced to live and primarily walled off from the remaining city. The Germans established at least 1,000 ghettos throughout German occupied Europe. The Germans regarded the ghettos as a temporary way to control and segregate the Jewish population while the Nazis in Berlin attempted to come up with ideas as to the fastest and most efficient means to eliminate the Jewish people. Some ghettos existed for only a few days, others for months or years.

Between the years of 1939 and 1942, concentration camps grew more and more. The camps were at first called labor camps where the prisoners', primarily Jewish prisoners, but also prisoners who were opposed to the Third Reich worked in fields and in factories and to produce goods for the Germans. These goods produced by all the prisoners were sold for money for the Germans. The Germans would give the prisoners little food and water. As the Germans conquered more and more of Europe, they created new concentration camps. The names of a few of some of the camps were: Dachau (1933), Gusen (1939), Neuengamme (1940), Gross-Rosen (1940), Auschwitz (1940), Natzweiler (1940), Stuffhof (1942), Majdanek (February 1943), and many, many more. These were just some of the concentration camps. Some of these camps were soon turned into death camps.

Dachau Concentration Camp was one of the first labor camps to be created. Dachau was the first camp for "political prisoners." During the first year, Dachau held about 4,800 prisoners: German Communists, Social Democrats, Trade Unionists, and other political opponents against the Third Reich Party. Later, other groups were placed in Dachau such as Jehovah's Witnesses, Gypsies, homosexuals, and criminals. Few Jews were in this camp, but later on in late 1938, more Jews were placed in Dachau. After Kristallnacht more than 10,000 Jewish men were placed into Dachau Concentration Camp.

Adolf Hitler created polite words to disguise the horrible crimes that he was planning to do. One of these words was the "Final Solution". Under the command of Hitler, the segregation and persecution of Jews started in stages. The "Final Solution" was the complete annihilation of the Jewish population. The German police began massive killing operations against the entire Jewish people. In 1941, the Germans created many ways to kill the Jews. One way they killed the Jews was by using mobile gas vans. Mobile gas vans were trucks that had exhaust pipes altered to pump monoxide gas into the truck, where the Jews would be locked up inside and killed from breathing in the dangerous fumes. They killed at least 152,000 people in the gas vans. Another way they killed the Jewish people was by shooting thousands among thousands of Jews and leaving them in pits in the forest. Later on, the citizens of the town began to complain about the smell of the corpses.

The Germans began to realize that they needed to hide the proof that they killed many thousands of Jews, political prisoners, Gypsies and more in the forests throughout Europe. Adolf Hitler then formed a unit of Nazis whose sole job was to get rid of the evidence: corpses. The Nazis were put in charge of Jews and any political prisoners and forced them to uncover these shallow, make shift graves of the exterminated people and throw them into crematoriums. These crematoriums were built inside vans so they could travel from one killing site to another to destroy any evidence of the Nazis' horrific crimes against humanity. After all of the corpses were burned and all the evidence was destroyed, the Nazis would then kill the remaining Jews who were used to exhume the bodies so as to leave no human alive to recount the disgusting details of the Nazis' mass extermination. These prisoners would then be thrown into these same crematoriums but they would still be alive.

Autumn of 1941, General Odilo Globocnik had another plan to systematically murder the Jews of the general population. The name for this was Operation Reinhard. This plan involved killing centers in Poland – Krakow, Belzec, Treblinka, Chelmno and Sobibor. The main purpose of this plan was to murder many Jews. In the gas chambers at Majdanek camp, the SS killed ten thousand Jews. Another camp was called Auschwitz II (Auschwitz-Birkenau) this was also built as a killing center; this camp killed approximately one million Jews. The German SS and police killed around

2,700,000 Jews in the killing camps with either poison gas or by shooting them. The "Final Solution" occurred all throughout Europe and successfully managed to annihilate 6 million Jews. The Nazis and Adolf Hitler's SS men were the people who were in charge of these mass murders.

Death Marches were very tough especially when you were starving or very ill and weak. A death march was a forced march of all of the prisoners, away from their current camp to escape the oncoming allied soldiers, to march over long distances and under horrible conditions to another camp. The prisoners were guarded heavily and treated brutally. Many died from mistreatment or were shot. If some of the prisoners were too slow or stopped to take a break, they would either be trampled to death or shot by an SS soldier. They would travel from one ghetto or concentration camp to another camp or ghetto or death camp. They were forced on these death marches to avoid the approaching enemies of the

Nazis, therefore, the Nazis had to evacuate some of the camps and make the prisoners walk and run on a march for miles upon miles to another camp. The primary reason for these death marches were because the SS men did not want one of the prisoners to escape to an enemy alive and tell their stories to the allies. Another reason was because the SS men needed their prisoners to continue to work to keep up the production of their weaponry. The last reason was because they thought that if they kept the Jewish people moving and separated from the rest of Europe, then maybe the Nazi regime would survive.

The situation throughout World War II became worse and worse for all the Jewish people throughout German occupied Europe. Not only the Jewish people, but also many other people's lives became worse. Starvation was prevalent throughout Europe and many people were joining the partisan groups in the forest trying to destroy the German army. The extermination camps were killing prisoners by the hundredths of thousands and there appeared to be no end in site. Death was the result from gas chambers, crematoriums, forced labor, starvation, brutality, execution, and exposure to extreme temperatures and diseases. Life just became harder and harder for everyone.

The people who survived the Holocaust are unbelievably strong. They stared death in the face and overcame all of the adversities to remain alive to tell their story, so that their families did not die in vain. The survivors' recount their stories for everyone to learn about the worst brutality that mankind can do to mankind. They want to teach everyone about history, so that no one will ever forget and it should never repeat itself or happen again. Naftali Schlomowitz is one of the few survivors from Lithuania and is an amazing man. He has experienced so much in his life and survived not only The Kovno Ghetto, Kovno Concentration Camp, but also Dachau Concentration Camp. He is the bravest and strongest person I know. My name is Nicole Schneider and Naftali Schlomowitz is my grandfather. He is my hero and this story is about his will to survive.

Chapter Two:

Life as they knew it changed forever during the summer of 1940. It was a Saturday; Naftali Schlomowitz was on the third floor of a clinic for a medical check-up. Suddenly, he heard tanks on the main street. Everyone in the clinic went out onto the street to watch.

It took three days and three nights for the Russian tanks to arrive in Kovno, Lithuania. Naftali was only fourteen years old. The people who supported the Russians posted flyers saying that the Lithuanian President, Antanas Smetona, ran away with suitcases filled with money. Later, Naftali's cousin, David Cotton, told Naftali what had happened in the suburb of Kovno.

David lived in a large primarily German community. David's parents, Shmuel and Chaya Cotton, owned a cosmetic store and photography studio. A German customer said to Shmuel that he was leaving to Germany and in one year from today he would return. He stated that when he came back, he was going to make Shmuel sweep the streets and he would be an officer giving Shmuel the orders.

Immediately after the Russian occupation, the new government began implementing political, economic and Soviet policies. On July 1, all cultural and religious organizations were closed. The Communist Party of Lithuania — with its 1,500 members, — were designated the only legitimate political party. All other youth groups and political parties including the Zionist party had to close their doors. The Soviets arrested about 2,000 of the most prominent political activists as to have no opposition to their government. All bank accounts with holdings over 1,000 litas (currency in Lithuania), real estate holdings larger than 1,800 sq ft, and private businesses with over 20 workers or grossing more than 150,000 *litas* were nationalized. All land was nationalized; the largest farms were reduced to 0.30 km^2, and extra land was distributed to small farmers. Farm taxes were increased by 50–200%. Some farmers were unable to pay these outrageous new taxes, and were put on trial. Approximately 12,000 individuals were arrested and thrown in prisons as enemies of the Communist Regime. Between June 14 and June 18, 1941, less than a week before the Nazi invasion, some 17,000 Lithuanians were deported to Siberia, where many died due to inhumane living conditions. Some of Naftali's family members who were considered wealthy were arrested by the Soviets and deported to Siberia labor camps. Naftali's cousins on his grandmother's side were arrested just a few weeks before the German's invaded. They spent their war years in several labor camps in Siberia but managed to survive under horrible conditions. ATLEAST THE SOVIETS DID NOT HAVE GAS CHAMBERS AND CREMATORIUMS!

Life for the Jews was definitely worse than their Lithuanian neighbors. The Soviets were strong Anti-Semites and they imposed stricter laws for the Jewish people of Lithuania. The Russians took over the properties of Jewish owned businesses. During the night, the Jewish owners were secretly sent to Siberia labor camps in Russia. Naftali's father, Zalman Schlomowitz worked as a printer at his brother-in-law's shop. When the Russians arrived they made Zalman a manager of two printing shops. His mother worked from home, covering metal buttons with fabric. These metal buttons were ordered from Germany, but once the Russians arrived, they were unable to order them anymore. After school, Naftali would go to a machine shop to make the metal buttons to help his mom with the family business.

As the months went on, more and more laws were enforced against the Jews. Naftali's family could no longer run a business and they were forced to fire their employee. Soon after Naftali was no longer allowed to attend his Hebrew school. These were just some of the many laws that were imposed by the Russians.

Anti-Semitism was becoming prevalent among the Lithuanians in the city where Naftali lived. One day Naftali was riding home on his bicycle, a gift he cherished from his parents and was hit by a Lithuanian driver. His bicycle was destroyed and this entire event was witnessed by a Lithuanian police officer. Since Naftali was Jewish and the driver was not, the police officer chose to disregard the entire accident and he was never compensated for his damaged bicycle.

In June, the Russians paid for children to go to the country to a summer camp, near the Baltic Sea, and Naftali was one of the lucky ones that went. They traveled by train from Kovno to Palanga, Lithuania and upon arrival there was a total of 600 children from different parts of Lithuania. They all stayed in cottages and played on the beach, just like a typical summer camp. Unlike most summer camps, these children watched the Russian troops build a wall to divide Lithuania in two. The Germans controlled one side and the Russians controlled the other.

WAR BROKE OUT BETWEEN GERMANY AND RUSSIA!!! June 22, 1941, Naftali was still away in Palanga, at sleep away camp. The German rockets were flying overhead, but the Russians did not have any rockets to retaliate. All the children had to take their belongings and walk along the beach. Naftali's suitcase was too heavy, they were all told to leave the suitcases and a truck would come later to get their belongings. The children were walking towards the Latvian border and saw rifles left on the ground by Russian soldiers that did not want to fight and had fled barefoot. The Russians left their shoes behind to be able to run faster. All the children, Naftali included, threw the rifles and shoes into the ocean so the Germans would not get them.

Later, Naftali saw seven German soldiers on bicycles with machine guns built into the bikes but thank goodness the soldiers ignored all the children.

The Germans biked in the direction where the sound of artillery was coming from. All of the 600 children arrived at a Latvian farm, where they all fit into a barn. There were no trucks available to take them away from the fighting. Everyone later had to go back to Palanga, which was under control by the Germans now. The Russians destroyed a wooden bridge and when they arrived the Germans were repairing the bridge.

There were orders for all the Jewish children to go to a bus terminal, about 100 to 150 of the children were Jewish. At the bus terminal, they encountered the entire Jewish population of Palanga there. The Germans were selecting adults and older children to go one direction while the smaller children and women were instructed to go the other way. Naftali hid with the younger children, which eventually saved his life.

The men and older children were taken to one synagogue and the women and younger children were taken to a different synagogue. A day later, the SS Germans were kicking all the men and older children out of the synagogue and throwing them onto trucks, from there they went directly to the forest and were forced to dig their own graves where they were shot to death. They were forced to line up in rows in front of the pits they just dug and were shot in the back. As they fell into the pits, the next row of people would line up and be shot in the back and they too would fall into the pits on top of the other bodies. In this gruesome fashion the SS Germans murdered all the Jewish men and older children from the town of Palanga. If Naftali had chosen to stay with the older boys, he would have been shot in the forest and he would have perished at the age of fourteen.

Three days later, the Germans took the women and children to a barn owned by a Lithuanian farmer and finally gave everyone some food to eat. Everyday the Germans took only the boys to the city to clean the German soldiers' rooms and then would bring the boys back late at night. A few days before Naftali was allowed to return home, the Germans took everyone into a cellar and Naftali was able to find his suitcase. His most valued treasures were still intact in his suitcase, much to his relief. The Red Cross arrived to the farm with buses, which Naftali's parents fortunately paid for him to ride home on. The Germans called out people's names from a list and those who were called were able to ride the bus back home. It was a sad day to see the faces left behind as their bus drove away from the farm. With great relief their parents were waiting for their children when they returned home. Naftali does not know what happened to the remaining women and children but one can only imagine.

Chapter Three:

It was a bittersweet reunion. Upon returning home, Naftali and his family had only a few days together in their house. While Naftali was held on a farm in Palanga praying to be reunited with his family, the Germans were hard at work establishing a ghetto in the poorest section of town. By the end of July 1941, The Germans ordered for all the Jews in Kovno to pack up their belongings and provided them with a list of what they were allowed to bring with them to the Ghetto. This list was very specific and included one dining room table per family, one chair per person, two plates each, one cup or glass each plus a saucer, one fork, one knife, one spoon each and containers for condiments. They were not allowed to bring with them any expensive dishes or any electric kitchen utensils. They were also allowed to take one bed per person, one set of bedding and three sets of sheets/pillowcases. As for the clothes, women were allowed four dresses, a winter and summer coat, three pairs of shoes and four sets of underwear. The men were allowed two suits, a summer and a winter coat, two pairs of shoes and four sets of underwear. The children up to age 14 were allowed to take all their children clothes and footwear; those over the age of 14 were allowed to take what the adults were allowed to take. They were not allowed to take any electronics such as radios but they were allowed to take equipment that helped them work but no machinery that was installed or any expensive equipment such as x-ray equipment. Once they were all packed, they needed to hire Lithuanians with carts and wagons, who charged them outrageous fees to help them move into the Ghetto.

They were forced to leave their homes with all their valuables left behind and relocate into the ghetto. The Jews in Kovno were forced to move into a ghetto in the town of Vilijampole-Slobodka. This was the poorest and most underdeveloped area of Lithuania with small wooden houses, inadequate plumbing facilities, no running water, no sewage system, no hospital, no homes for the aged and the orphans and most definitely not large enough to hold the entire Jewish population of Kovno. Before the war, it accommodated twelve thousand people and now it was to hold close to thirty thousand citizens. When the Ghetto opened, no one was responsible to assign homes, everyone needed to find somewhere to live. Those that had some money tried to buy a place from the Lithuanians that were moving out. Families were forced to double and triple up into single-family homes. Unfortunately, the poorer people were unable to find any room at all and had to live in the streets.

Fortunately for Naftali and his family, his Grandmother on his father's side owned a house in the Ghetto and they moved in with her. Naftali was one of three siblings. He had an older brother, Meier and a younger sister, Tzipora. They were not the only family members to move in with his Grandmother. Both of Naftali's parents, Rosa and Zalman had six siblings with children of their own. Naftali's Aunt Chaya Koton on his mother's side, moved in with her husband, Shmuel and their son David with their Aunt and Uncle Shimon and Ethel Zalsberg. On his father's side, Uncle Motel with his wife Luba and their two daughters Hanetkeh and Munkha moved in with Aunt Bella, Aunt Mena with her two daughters and Aunt Tsila with her daughter. Aunt Bella was not married. Aunt Tsila's husband, Sandler and his parents were brutally murdered by Lithuanians while they worked in their bakery, just after the Germans invaded Lithuania. Sandler managed to write the words "Revenge" on the wall, in his own blood. (Photo at the end of the book.) Aunt Mena's husband, Abrasha Burstein went into hiding alone and left his family behind, what a coward!

Inside the Ghetto, On August 4th, 1941 Jewish Council of Elders known as the "Altestenrat" was formed based on German orders. The council's duties were to oversee and run the day-to-day life of the Ghetto and to carry out the German decrees. The members of the council were prominent Jewish leaders who were involved in the Jewish community before the Ghetto was erected. The chairman of the council was Elkhanan Elkes, a popular physician and one of Kovno's most respected Jewish citizens. Their first line of business was to establish the Jewish Ghetto Police to protect the citizens inside the ghetto and to implement the decrees from the Germans and the Altestenrat. It was not easy to recruit volunteers to join the Jewish police, as no one was certain what exactly their role would be under the German Government. Once the ghetto was closed the police had to deal with the horrible housing crisis and lack of homes to accommodate all 30,000 residents. Food distribution was overseen by the police as well as ensuring everyone showed up for their daily work assignments. The police were responsible for judging any criminal or civil cases that occurred among the Jews. The police even had to follow and carry out orders from the Germans such as rounding up the Jewish people for labor brigades, participating with the Nazis in inspections at the ghetto gate to catch people from smuggling in food or wood for fuel and even at times assisting the Nazis when it came time for selections to down size the population inside the ghetto. The police became very unpopular amongst the citizens in the ghetto. At times, the ghetto police would even use violence in order to carry out the German decrees. They were viewed as working alongside the Germans and were protected from the selection and deportation processes that would occur at random throughout the ghetto. The ghetto police were quite aware of the resentment towards them but insisted that without force they would not be respected, feared or obeyed and therefore there would be no order inside the ghetto.

The Jews inside the ghetto prayed that life inside the ghetto would be better than life outside the ghetto even with the Jewish police. Once the Germans pushed the Russians out of Lithuania, the Pro-Nazi Lithuanians terrorized the defenseless Jewish population of Kovno. These men would roam the streets to beat, rob, humiliate, arrest and murder the Jews while Lithuanian neighbors looked on and offered no assistance. On the night of June 26th 1941, over one thousand Jews were butchered in the most savage of ways. These ruthless barbarians would crash children's heads with the butts of their guns and then tear their heads off. They would repeatedly throw people into brick walls and telephone poles. They massacred entire families in their own apartments. They even sawed off a Rabbi's head and cut out the tongue and pocked out the eyes of the leader of the Jewish Yeshiva from Villiampole. The following day dozens of Jews were forced to gather in the courtyard of a garage in the center of the city. These Jews were brutally beaten and killed with shovels, steel rods and iron bars while the Lithuanian community looked on, cheered and photographed the entire barbaric event. It was estimated that ten thousand Jews were murdered between June and July of 1941. The Jewish community now hoped that even though they had to live in poverty and under primitive conditions that they would be left alone by the Lithuanians and the Germans.

Unfortunately, the peace that the Jewish community dreamed of did not come into being. On August 18, 1941, just three days after the ghetto was closed off from the world, the Germans demanded that the "Altestenrat" provide them with well-educated professionals to report to work in the city's archives performing clerical work. Five hundred and fifty people were ordered to appear for work but instead of going to work they were all shot to death. These murdered Jews were some of Kovno's top musicians, engineers, economists, artists, journalists, and lawyers. The community was in shock! The next day, the Germans began performing house-to-house searches for the next five weeks in order to rob the

Jews of any valuables they might have brought with them into the ghetto. Along with these robberies continued beatings, torture and murder.

The Germans sent a decree that within the next few weeks all the inmates of the ghetto had to hand over all their money, gold, silver, jewelry and other valuables. They were only allowed to keep ten marks per family. Jews were also not allowed to own any electrical appliances, musical instruments, bicycles and cameras. When Naftali moved into the ghetto he smuggled in with him his beloved camera. He loved taking photos and cared for his camera. He hid his camera in his Grandmother's attic, in the ceiling floorboards. Naftali's father knew about the camera and where it was hidden and ordered Naftali to bring the camera to the Germans. He insisted that Naftali was risking the entire family's life if he did not turn over the camera. Understanding how dangerous it was to not follow a German decree and not willing to risk the lives of his entire family, Naftali retrieved his camera and unwillingly handed it over to the Germans.

New decrees were issued on a regular basis. The Germans ordered the Jews to hand over suits, fur, leather, furniture and any objects of art. If these orders were not followed then death was to be expected!! The greatest offense was hiding weapons. Even weapons that were used in plays for props such as swords and daggers were an offense to keep. People lost their lives for keeping them. If hidden weapons were found, all the residents of that house and even of the block faced the death penalty.

Chapter Four:

The Ghetto was held in two sections; a "Large Ghetto" and a "Small Ghetto" divided by Paneriu Street, where Christian wagons and cars would pass underneath. Eventually a small bridge was built to connect the two parts of the Ghetto. Many of Naftali's Aunts, Uncles and Cousins lived in the small ghetto as the Grandmother's house was filled to capacity. By August 15, 1941, the ghetto was sealed off with barbed wire around its boundary and armed guards patrolling the gates, imprisoning 30,000 Jewish citizens from Kovno. The only way to leave the ghetto was through work, where the German or the Lithuanian guards would escort the Jews to places of work and then back again to the ghetto. It was mandated that all men between the ages of 14 and 60 and all women between the ages of 15 and 55 were obligated to work. The only exception was for women with small children at home. Everyday including Sundays, Naftali and his family members who were required to work, would go to the town square near the main gate for 5am where the Germans took count and would organize and assign the laborers into work groups. Their workday would not end until 8:00 pm. As the Jews left the ghetto to their various places of work, they were forced to walk on the street, with the armed German or Lithuanian guards walking on the sidewalk. Every Jewish person had a yellow star on his or her chest and on his or her back. As a matter of principle, Jews were not allowed to walk anywhere but on the street, with the horses. The yellow star had to be worn on one's clothes at all times, and a German or Lithuanian was to guard the Jews at all times. Throughout the day, the Germans would patrol the Ghetto making sure everyone was at work. As time went by, the Germans took advantage of those who remained in the Ghetto by rounding up certain people for executions. Those who were outside the gates working were safer and less likely to be seized than those who stayed inside the gates.

First Naftali was assigned to the train station to unload coal from incoming trains. He thought this was exhausting work until he was assigned to the military airfield in Aleksotas on September 8, 1941. This airport was badly damaged by German bombs when they attacked Russia and was in desperate need of repair and expansion. The military airport was the least desirable place to work. The work consisted of heavy, physical labor and it was done outdoors, no matter the weather conditions. It was a three and a half mile march to the airfield everyday with an exhausting twelve-hour shift before returning back to the Ghetto and marching another three and a half miles. The German High Command made certain the Jews worked day and night; a total of four thousand Jewish workers worked within a 24-hour period everyday in this military airfield. Naftali had to dig up the destroyed concrete runways, push trolleys, and carry 50-pound bags of cement, stones, bricks, and iron in strong winds, severe frosts and heavy rain. The work was exhausting but it was made much worse by the beatings they would get if they stopped working. Guards armed with rifles and supervisors armed with whips oversaw the work. The winters were brutally cold and with only rags for clothes, they needed to continue to work regardless of the weather.

On October 27, 1941, Naftali, his Uncle Shmuel Koton and his cousin David Koton were all working at the military airfield and were forced to stay for the next 12-hour shift, as the night shift never arrived. When they finally returned back to the Ghetto, the morning of October 28th, 1941, they were told to go immediately to Demokratu Square. There they met up with their entire family; scared, hungry and exhausted they remained in the square for the entire day and well into the night. Helmet Rauca, the Gestapo Sergeant in charge of the Ghetto mandated that all the Jews in the Ghetto were to assemble by 6:00am in Demokratu Square, anyone found in their home would be shot immediately. He did promise the Jewish Council that this was merely a head count of the population and from there they were planning on dividing the residents into heavy laborers and others. This was a complete and utter lie! Everyone stood in this Square throughout the day and into the night with no food or water. People around them were dying from exhaustion, dehydration and starvation. They waited their turn to pass in front of Helmet Rauca, who sent them to the right or to the left with a wave of his finger on the basis of their appearance or some other trivial reason. Upon being chosen to go to the right, also known as the "bad side", the beatings would begin by the Nazis. They would kick the Jews with their boots, beat them with their fists, their rifle butts and their sticks, they would whip them and stab them with daggers. This would continue until the Jews would collapse and then finally they would be dragged away by the other "chosen" Jews. Naftali's father's sister, Bella and Shmuel Koton's sister were helping Aunt Ethel and Uncle Shimon Zalsberg to walk in front of Helmet Rauca as they were older and were having trouble walking after standing for so many hours. Rauca sent them all to the right. These two young women were chosen to go to the wrong side just because they were helping two elderly family members. Naftali's father attempted to save his sister and offered Rauca a gold Parker pen in exchange for his sister, Bella. Helmet Rauca took the pen but never spared Bella. She remained on the "bad" side and was never seen again. By the end of this selection process, 9,200 people were removed from the Large Ghetto and placed in the Small Ghetto. No one in the Small Ghetto knew what his or her fate might be. They believed they were being relocated and taken to other quarters.

Approximately four kilometers from the Ghetto was a fortress by the name of The Ninth Fort. It was built in the late 19th century and was used as a prison and a holding station for prisoners being transported to labor camps during the Russian occupation of Lithuania. Once the Germans defeated the Russians, it became a place of torture and mass executions. Some 25,000 of Kovno's Jews, as well as 15,000 Jews deported from across Europe including thousands of Jewish Prisoners-of-War who had served in the Red Army, and many other Jews were murdered there. Single and mass arrests, as well as "Actions" in the Ghetto, almost always ended with a "death march" to the Ninth Fort. The road that led uphill towards the Ninth Fort from the ghetto was nicknamed by the Nazis as "The Way to Heaven".

Rumors started to spread throughout the Small Ghetto that the prisoners of war in the Ninth Fort were digging deep ditches. No one wanted to believe the worst and in the morning of October 29th, 1941, the Jewish citizens marched quietly out of the Small Ghetto without resisting towards the Ninth Fort. When the people realized they were being marched to their death some tried to escape but were shot and killed immediately with their bodies left on the side of the roads and fields. Upon arriving at the Ninth Fort, they were forced to undress and stand naked in the cold for hours upon hours. The children were thrown into the ditches first, followed by the women who were shot with automatic rifles and machine guns while standing at the edge of the ditch, the men were saved for last. Some of them were buried alive to save on the bullets.

This "Great Action" killed 30 percent of the ghetto population. Only 17,000 people remained alive in the ghetto. There was not a family inside the ghetto that had not lost a family member. Naftali's family was paralyzed with grief and shock. No one believed that work was the way to survive. A great amount of people that were selected for death were strong, young laborers. They could not understand what rhyme or reason was behind the selection process. No one had faith in the Gestapo's promises that this was the last "action" and that there would be no more as long as everyone would work they would be left alone. The Gestapo Commander, Helmet Rauca and Captain Fritz Jordan, the "expert" on Jewish Affairs for the German civil administration tried hard to bring the moral up in the ghetto by giving the Jewish Council a 10,000 Reichmark check to be distributed to those working in the military airport. Even with all their promises and money, the will to go on was hopeless.

Chapter Five:

Before the Great Action occurred, there was another action, which took place on October 4, 1941 in the Small Ghetto. Everyone from the "Small Ghetto" was liquidated and taken to the Ninth Fort where they were shot to death and thrown into pits, just like the Great Action of October 28th. Prior to their death, the Jews were forced to dig trenches in the hospital courtyard. The factory workers from a fur factory outside the Ghetto watched from the other side of the fence as the Nazis threw the sick seniors from the old age home, and all the small children from the orphanage into these trenches. Then at 1:00pm the infectious disease hospital inside the small ghetto was completely destroyed. The Germans bordered up the doors with wood and nails while all the staff, patients and visitors were trapped inside the hospital. The Germans then set the entire building on fire. Everyone in the Ghetto watched in horror as the hospital burned all day and all night as smoke filled the air. No one was allowed to try to put out the flames. Kovno Ghetto had their own Jewish Ghetto firefighters and all they could do was watch in desperation as innocent lives were burned up in such a horrific fashion. It was incomprehensible!! With this action the small ghetto lost half their population, approximately one thousand, eight hundred people perished during that action. There was no hospital left in the ghetto and all medical personal that were not in the hospital that day, signed up for forced labor in the brigades or tried to learn a new trade in order to disassociate themselves from the medical profession.

After both these terrible "Great Actions", life had to go on inside the walls of the ghetto. Winter was quickly approaching and the winters in Lithuania were unbearably cold and bitter! The winter of 1941-1942 was the coldest winter on record in Kovno. Trying to find wood for fuel was impossible and it was even harder to try to smuggle firewood into the ghetto. The ghetto residents were forced to demolish houses and wooden fences for fuel. The chief of the German ghetto guard prohibited houses or parts of houses or fences from being demolished but the inmates defied the prohibition stating they would rather be shot to death than freeze to death. Naftali recalls being so cold that it was even difficult to breath.

The lack of food was another never-ending problem. There was a vegetable garden along the river inside the ghetto, but it did not provide enough food. Primarily, all the food needed to come from outside the ghetto and the only legal supply was from the German civil administration that provided ration cards to the ghetto inhabitants after their long days at work. "The Altestenrat" established a branch under their supervision known as the Ghetto's Food Supply Office. This office was responsible for distributing the food rations provided from the Germans to the people in the ghetto. The ghetto inmates received half the ration that the Lithuanians received and even the Lithuanians rations were minimal secondary to wartime rations. These rations that were provide to the Jews were one-third of the minimum calories required for daily survival. The meat, when it was provided was mainly horsemeat, tough and chewy. The Germans made sure to always remove a portion from the ghetto's rations for themselves which left the inmates with much less food then promised. The food that was distributed to the people inside the Ghetto was meager, 200 grams of bread per person per day, 100 grams of horsemeat once in two weeks, and occasionally, a kilogram of potatoes

The potatoes that were delivered to the ghetto were mostly rotten potatoes but this did not matter. Naftali remembers his mother gladly taking the family's portion of rotten potatoes and using the entire batch of rotten potatoes including the peel to make soup. This thin, watery soup was called "The Yushnik". One day, Shmuel Koton, Naftali's uncle, came home with live rabbits. Naftali was the rabbits' primary caretaker and would go to the fields and find scraps of food such as the tops of carrots that people would throw away and bring it home for the rabbits to eat. The rabbits had babies and multiplied. His uncle then killed and skinned the rabbits for food. The meat was tough and tasted like grass, it was not something Naftali wanted to eat but his family insisted he needed to eat it to try to keep up his strength.

Poverty was very prevalent in the ghetto and virtually the entire ghetto population was impoverished. After the "Great Action" of October 1941, a Welfare Office was established; this office was another branch that was formed under the supervision of the Jewish Council, "The Altestenrat". The Germans gave "The Altestenrat" the possessions of those victims that were killed during the Great Action and had no remaining family. Of course, the Germans distributed the items after they chose what they wanted to keep for themselves. The Welfare office then distributed the clothing to those needy individuals and airfield workers who needed to work outdoors in the cold winter months. The office was also able to provide the poor with a little firewood during the cold winter months. On April 8, 1942, the Welfare Office opened a soup kitchen. This kitchen distributed 800 meager bowls of warm soup a day. This would be the only warm food of the day for the hungry and poor people of the ghetto. Accepting help from the Welfare office was a humiliating and degrading experience especially for those individuals who were the working middle class prior to the war. The Welfare office tried to be as discreet as possible when offering assistance.

The lack of housing was also a never-ending problem. One would think that after the Great Actions where one third of the ghetto inmates were lost, the remaining inmates would all have been able to find housing. This was not the case as the Germans constantly kept reducing the size of the ghetto. "The Altestenrat" then formed another branch under their supervision known as The Housing Office. They were in charge of the task of finding a roof over everyone's head. When the ghetto was reduced in size, the remaining residents would have to go to the Housing Office to ask for assistance with relocating to an area inside the ghetto walls as the Germans confiscated their home. The remaining ghetto continued to consist of multiple families forced to live together in small, wooden single-family homes. As hard as the Housing Office worked, the issue of overcrowding was always a problem.

The overcrowded living situation, the inadequate nutrition and the never-ending poverty all created a difficult situation for the ghetto's Health Office. This office was yet another branch formed and supervised by "The Altestenrat". Due to the poor living conditions and overcrowding in the ghetto rapid spreading of epidemics, especially typhoid, was endangering all of the inhabitants. The sick were scared to ask for medical help for fear of being discovered by the Germans. They were too sick to leave the ghetto to work and of course because they did not work they did not receive their food ration cards and were also unable to smuggle food into the ghetto. Therefore, the sick person was doomed to death. In response, the Health Office initially established a secret underground hospital due to the destruction of the hospital in the "Small Ghetto". It was with great fear and hesitation that The Health Office finally opened a new hospital in the "Large Ghetto". The office saw no other option than to establish a new hospital for fear if diseases started to spread inside the ghetto walls, it would give the Germans an excuse to kill the remaining ghetto inmates to stop the spread of disease. The Health Office made sure there was no maternity ward in the hospital since pregnancy was made a capital offence and punishable by death and there was also no infectious disease ward, since the Germans feared infectious diseases the most. When patients needed to be admitted with typhus or some other dreaded disease they would be treated under some other medical name or treated in their home for their own safety. Thanks to the remaining medical staff and the Health Office, Kovno Ghetto never suffered from any real epidemics.

Chapter Six:

From the end of 1941, after the "Big Action" in October 28, 1941, there was a relatively "quiet" period in the ghetto lasting for approximately 22 months. During this time, although there were almost no big "actions", there was still torture, starvation, slave labor, misery, and plenty of killings. There continued to have "small actions"; like the Stalingrad Action where 44 ghetto Jews were killed at the Ninth Fort for supposedly illegal smuggling occurred, but in truth it was retaliation for the Germans surrendering in Stalingrad. The battle of Stalingrad was important to Hitler because its capture would secure the left side of the German armies and would cut off fuel to Stalin's war machine. Joseph Stalin and Hitler were complete enemies and when Stalin figured out what was happening, he sent the strongest men, who were able to hold a rifle, go out and defend the city.

The Germans continued with their decrees and prohibitions, but even with all the above mentioned abuse, from this time period until September 1943 was considered a normal period inside the ghetto. Where normal meant having just enough food to avoid starvation and death, where people were shot but the community still existed, where there was no mass executions but life continued behind barbed wire with slave labor and without any rest or relaxation.

Naftali's brother, Meier was planning his wedding with his long time girlfriend, Bella. Meier worked at nights to earn money; after his 12-hour shift of labor where he would earn his food ration cards, he would then dig tunnels for people in their homes. These people were trying to build safe rooms and hiding places for themselves and their family so they would be prepared when the next action would occur. When Meier earned enough money, he bought a chicken to give to the Rabbi to pay for their wedding. Bella and Meier got married the spring of 1943, during the period of relative quiet.

Education was always very important for the Jews of Kovno but with all the Great Actions and instability inside the Ghetto, no one had time to think about their children's education. By the end of 1941, during the relative quiet period "The Altestenrat" formed another branch under their supervision called The Education Office. Their responsibility was the registration of all school age children regardless of the fact that they lacked teachers, books or firewood. Unfortunately, not many children remained alive after the actions and those that were alive needed to stay home to watch their younger siblings since their parents needed to work 12-hour shifts. Even under these tough conditions, two schools were established with approximately two hundred students in each school. Even though the schools were cramped and filled with children of all ages and level of education, the schools still managed to challenge the children's intellect and provided a diversion from their horrible life in the ghetto. These students managed to put on a holiday show for their parents and other ghetto inmates and for just a little while: everyone forgot about their miserable lives and enjoyed that small moment of happiness and pleasure.

The Education Office was even able to run a ghetto library until February 1942, when the Germans confiscated all books in the ghetto, including holy prayer books, no matter what language. The Germans announced collection spots for all books and provided a deadline. Just like the night of Kristallnacht, once again the Germans collected books to burn. They burnt books that were either not written by Pure Germans, had to do with homosexuals and other religions, and they burnt books that were "against" the Nazi regime. The Nazis would throw the books also written by Jews into a massive fire and would watch as the books were scorched to ashes. Many books were destroyed for no reason and many were devastated watching their books being turned into ashes. The burning of the books caused the ghetto library to close.

After the deadline, the Germans conducted house searches and if any books were found, the punishment was severe and usually ended with torture and eventually death. This "Book Action" was quite devastating for the children's education but none as devastating as closing the schools. Unfortunately, by August 1942, the Germans demanded the schools to be closed. The only schools allowed to remain open were the vocational schools. According to thefreedictionary.com "Vocational schools are schools that offer instruction and practical introductory experience in skilled trades such as mechanics, carpentry, plumbing, and construction." The Education Office decided to work around the German's decree and added regular school subjects to the vocational schools curriculum. When there was a will, there was a way!

As hard as it was to imagine, cultural activities began to form in the ghetto even with severe official restrictions. There were literary lectures, choral performances from the children in the vocational schools, and religious study groups who continued to study Torah. During the summer of 1942, the ghetto police formed an orchestra with thirty-five instrumentalists and five singers. Approximately 80 concerts were performed over the course of the ghetto's existence. In the beginning, with most inmates still mourning from the loss of family and friends, many found the idea of entertainment in any form disrespectful to the lives that had been lost. They felt it was wrong to hold concerts in what was now a permanent place of mourning. The first concert opened with a moment of silence, followed by 'Kol Nidre', which is the opening prayer and the name for the evening service that begins Yom Kippur. Finally, the remainder of the program consisted of serious and solemn music. The early objections gradually disappeared as inmates recognized the value of music for mourning and remembering, as well as for raising morale. Convinced of the importance of music for survival, the inmates began to forget where they were for one night, allowing them to leave the ghetto and go to a totally different world, at least in their imagination. In addition to musical performances, a large number of songs were composed and sung in the ghetto, many of them consisted of new lyrics set to pre-existing melodies. The songs expressed the suffering, hope, and despair of the inmates.

Chapter Seven:

There were approximately 17,000 Jews left in the Ghetto. Although nearly half the Jews in the Ghetto had been killed, the Germans continued to demand the same amount of workers appear for labor as usual. Naftali continued to work in the military airport until the end of 1942 when he was much too weak to continue this type of labor. Naftali went to the "The Altestenrat" to plead for another job. At this time, the Lithuanians were now working for the Third Reich in the front and the jobs in Kovno were left vacant. The Germans now needed the Jewish laborers to fill the shortage felt in a variety of businesses throughout Kovno. Approximately 150 various "city brigades" were developed and the ghetto inmates now filled these jobs. Treatment in general was far more humane in these city brigades than working in the military airport. The other advantage to working in these brigades was the ability to obtain food by bartering with the civilians in the community and smuggling it back into the ghetto. When they worked out in the military airport there were no civilians present which did not provide them with opportunities to barter for food.

Along with the increased opportunities to work in the city came opportunities to work inside the ghetto when the Germans opened workshops. The head of "The Altestenrat", Elkhanan Elkes, took advantage of the Germans and created ghetto workshops to provide work for those residents who would never have endured the backbreaking work of the labor brigade particularly the women, children and elderly. Knowing full well that an essential way for survival was work, the Jewish Council and Elkhanan Elkes hoped the Germans would not kill the Jews who were working and producing for their army. Eventually, these workshops employed close to four thousand five hundred people. These workshops ran day and night providing all the profits for the Germans. The Germans provided the necessary materials for these workshops. For example, one workshop worked to repair and sort through clothing and valuables that were taken from the Jews of Kovno, living and dead.

For a year and a half, Naftali was able to train in the vocational school; since he was young, the Jewish Council gave their permission for him to learn how to weld sheet metal, which could be used later inside the ghetto to fix machines such as sewing machines. He was already experienced with sewing machines since before the war, Naftali's family owned sewing machines and Naftali would repair them. He was then transferred to work in the "Werkstatten" workshop inside the ghetto as the workload increased and they needed the manpower. Naftali was therefore able to receive a permit paper from "The Altestenrat". This workshop was known for repairing and cleaning German Soldiers 'coats, uniforms and boots to be returned to the front line. Naftali remembers unloading truckloads of damaged and dirty German uniforms and shoes/boots from the war front. He needed to repair and sew these uniforms, then pack them back up and return the boxes to the front. It was also necessary for him to sew a second layer of fabric in the German soldiers' coats, as the Germans were needed to fight the battles in Russia where the winters were very cold. Due to the thickness of these coats, the sewing machines' needle plates would constantly breakdown.

Frustrated with the constant breaking down of these needle plates, Naftali approached Mr. Fisher, the mechanic manager in charge of the "Werkstatten" and suggested an improvement to the sewing machines. Mr. Fisher immediately agreed to allow Naftali to repair and modify these sewing machines. Naftali was able to modify the domestic sewing machines into industrial machines so the needle plates would no longer breakdown when the fabric was too thick. He used his knowledge that he learned from his days in the vocational school regarding sheet metal welding. He was able to fabricate a new needle plate by welding thicker metal to the needle plates. Mr. Fisher tried in vain to fix these needle plates himself and after 2 days it would breakdown again and again. Once, Naftali welded these new plates with reinforced metal, the needle plates no longer broke down. The ghetto inmates were now able to meet their quota of repaired coats without the delay of constantly fixing and replacing the needle plates of their sewing machines. What a relief to the workshop manager and all the inmates working inside the workshop. Mr. Fisher, the mechanic manager, was thrilled and insisted that Naftali continue to work with him. Naftali was then permanently placed in the machine shop in the "Werkstatten". Naftali remembers fixing sewing machines that were filled with cooking oil and he needed to place the machines into large pots of boiling water to allow the oil to pour out. He was able to repair all types of mechanical problems on all types of sewing machines such as hand knitting machines, motorized sewing machines and machines that were needed to repair boots and shoes. He was able to stay and work in the "Werkstatten" until the ghetto was liquated in July 1944.

Naftali's mother, Rosa was able to also work in the "Werkstatten" sewing and repairing the German uniforms, coats and boots. When Naftali's family moved into the ghetto, they managed to bring in a sewing machine with them. They managed to hide and keep their sewing machine throughout their ghetto life. Since they owned their own sewing machine and Rosa was familiar with using the machine, she was given permission from "The Altestenrat" to work inside the ghetto in the "Werkstatten". It was the only way to be able to obtain a job in the "Werkstatten" as it was deemed a good place to work. The Germans and Lithuanians did not oversee the day to day routine of these workshops, which allowed for a little less abuse and slightly more freedom.

Chapter Eight:

Starvation was the way of life for all the inhabitants inside the ghetto; so there was no surprise that the black market was developed and was so successful. The black market in the Kovno Ghetto was where people would sell extra food or jewels, gold, and other valuable items that they either had or smuggled in through the gates of the ghetto. Money was hard to come by, so the Jews exchanged gold coins, clothes, household items and anything else that the non-Jews outside the Ghetto were willing to take, in exchange for food. They would then sell the food in secret to those who needed the extra food for their families. In return they would receive gold, jewelry, and any other household items, which they would then be able to trade outside of the ghetto for more food and supplies they needed. The entire black market was based on supplies smuggled into the ghetto by those who worked outside the ghetto during the day. Those who were caught trading were executed immediately because it was illegal to trade.

Naftali's family was unable to survive on the small rations that the German's distributed. Luckily, when Naftali's family packed up their belongings to move into the ghetto, they packed up a 25-kilo bar of soap that they used to wash their clothes with. Naftali's father, Zalman purchased this bar of soap when he was in Paris before the war and before the move into the ghetto. Now that they were in the ghetto, they used the soap to trade for bread. They would slice apiece off from the bar of soap and trade the soap with the Lithuanians for bread, butter or meat. Naftali's family lived near the fence that separated the Jews from the Lithuanians. The Lithuanians would come to the fence and would ask, "Would you like to trade for bread?" On two occasions, Naftali traded soap for bread by throwing the packaged soap over the fence. The last time he attempted to trade for bread, the Lithuanian took the soap but threw over a package with a rock inside, he cheated Naftali out of the bread. Naftali was very upset and never traded for bread over the fence again.

His family had to resort to smuggling food into the ghetto. When Naftali's family moved into the ghetto, they also packed with them sheets and various paint colors. Naftali, his brother Meier and his father Zalman would cut the sheets into squares to make kerchiefs. Then they would paint red, blue and green flowers on these kerchiefs. Naftali's father worked as a printer outside the ghetto, in the city of Kovno, for the Germans. He had contact with the local population and therefore had the opportunity to trade these kerchiefs with the Christian women for food such as bread, butter and meat. Thank goodness Naftali's family was smart enough to pack extra sheets as well as paints to bring with them inside the ghetto. The women really liked these kerchiefs and the extra food Zalman acquired from trading these kerchiefs was able to sustain his family. Of course, he still needed to smuggle the food inside the ghetto, which was a challenge all on its own.

Zalman risked his life on a daily basis to smuggle food to his family because the Nazis regarded smuggling a capital offense. Returning to the Ghetto at night was an ordeal. Again, he would walk slowly in a group, accompanied by armed German soldiers. This time, however, they would be stopped at the gate to be searched. Even after people had managed to get some bread or a few potatoes, while risking their lives, there was no guarantee that they would succeed in delivering it to their hungry family members. On entering the ghetto there was no certainty that one could enter it safely. Often people were deprived here not only of their hard gotten food but also their very lives. The ghetto gates were always the most dangerous place there. Often brutal Germans killed people for little reason. They killed if numbers of those that were sent to work were insufficient or because a guard did not like the way Jews were passing through the gates. They even killed for no reason at all - by shooting into a crowd of people who simply happened to be there. The Jewish Police, who were at the gate occasionally, would allow a small amount of food for personal use, but anything beyond this was confiscated.

The normal procedure upon arriving at the gates at the end of the workday was that just before the gate, one would have to take off their hat, open their bag and raise their hands so the guards could check them. Naftali's father had a clever idea that allowed him to trick the guards. He would open his coat and raise his arms, holding his hat in one hand. They never found anything on him. After the search, he would take the bread, butter or meat out of his hat and bring the smuggled food home to his family. Occasionally, he would hide the food in his coat pocket. He had deep pockets and his coat was bulky so he managed to get the food by the guards without being caught. Naftali's family never dealt with the Ghetto's Black Market. It was much too risky and dangerous and they preferred not to take any unnecessary chances. It was tough enough to stay alive in the ghetto without looking for ways to get in trouble with the German guards.

Chapter Nine:

Naftali's father joined the Ghetto Police in order to be able to better protect his family and to be able to obtain food. It was easier to smuggle and trade for food with a Police uniform. The Germans had issued a decree that no one was allowed within two feet of the ghetto fence. The only exception was the Ghetto Police. Naftali's father would use the opportunity as a police officer to quietly trade items for food through the fence with the Lithuanians. This was another means of providing food for his family, as the rations were not enough to sustain a human being.

Another advantage to being a Ghetto Police Officer was the fact that the Nazis would notify the Ghetto Police in advance of any "Actions" that were going to take place. This would provide Naftali's father the opportunity and the time to prepare his family. One "Action" was called "The Kinder Action" where the Nazis were going door to door and house-to-house collecting all the children and removing them from the ghetto. One thousand three hundred children mostly under the age of twelve were dragged from their homes and killed in the Ninth Fort. Naftali's father, Zalman, prepared the family for what was to come and hid Aunt Mena's two daughters, ages three and five, Aunt Tsila's daughter who was four years old and his own daughter, Tzipora who was fourteen but very short and therefore presumed much younger, between the walls in the attic. Naftali's family built this hiding spot in their home to be used during "Actions". They were told to remain there in complete silence. If they were not prepared for this search, they would have clearly been removed and sent to their deaths at the Ninth Fort with the rest of the children that were rounded up that day.

From time to time, the Nazis would do random house searches and remove people from their homes for deportation. Naftali's father would stand in front of their house and when the Nazis approached the house to begin their search, he notified them that this house was already searched. Since Zalman was in Police uniform and was a Ghetto Police Officer, the Nazis believed him and skipped over their family's home. In this manner, Zalman managed to protect his immediate family and remaining members of his family during these "Actions"; wife, two sons, daughter, grandmother as well as his two sister-in-laws and three nieces managed to all stay alive throughout their years in the ghetto. Unfortunately, Zalman was unable to protect those family members that were not living with him in the Grandmother's house.

One day, during these random house searches, Naftali witnessed a mother not allowing a Nazi to take her child. The mother struggled with the Nazi, but unfortunately he was stronger than the mother and managed to grab the child. When he took the child out of the mother's arms, he proceeded to throw the child into the brick wall. The child died instantly. Images such as these have been permanently seared into Naftali's memory. How does one move on from witnessing such a gruesome crime? How does the mother continue on with her own life after witnessing the brutal death of her own flesh and blood?

One way the Jewish population inside the ghetto continued to persevere was through their involvement with the underground organizations, such as the Communist Anti-Fascist Organization and the Zionist Youth Movements. There were many different parties when the ghetto was first formed and each party had their basic differences. The Zionist groups were more popular with the Jews inside the ghetto and the communist groups had better contacts with the underground outside the ghetto. But by the summer of 1943 they all decided to combine forces and join into one organization: a united front with one goal, to destroy the Germans. They formed the Jewish General Fighting Organization, which consisted of men and women armed with illegal weapons obtained from the black market, all hoping to plan their escape.

The Jewish General Fighting Organization received help from "The Altestenrat". They supplied the members with money to buy weapons, to bribe the guards and to buy transportation. Even the Ghetto Jewish Police helped the underground with smuggling in weapons and people in and out of the ghetto. The ghetto police helped with weapon training and helped them to find the appropriate clothing for escaping into the forest. Slowly, leading members of the ghetto police started joining the underground. The Jews that worked in the ghetto workshops managed to smuggle out German uniforms to help the resistance fighters with their disguise. They not only smuggled German uniforms out of the workshops but they smuggled warm clothing out as well to help the fighters once they were in the forest.

The first attempt for the members of the underground to join the partisans occurred October

28, 1943, when 43 members left Kovno in an attempt to reach the forest and join the Partisans, also known as The Resistance Fighters. Unfortunately, only two men successfully reached the forest and met up with the Partisans, the remaining members were captured; all but 11 people were killed. The months between November 1943 and March 1944 were busy months for members of the underground attempting to escape and join the Partisans. Naftali's grade school friend, Moshe Abramovitz, told Naftali that he was escaping to the forest and tried to encourage Naftali to join him. Naftali refused to leave his family behind and therefore remained in the ghetto until liquidation. Unfortunately, only a little more than three hundred people were successful in reaching the forest and joining their Partisan unit to fight the Germans. Now, one can say, at least three hundred escaped the mass deportations that occurred in July 1944 although seventy of them died in battle.

The Nazis became suspicious of this underground movement and heard rumors that the Jewish Police were assisting them. Therefore, on March 26, 1944, the Nazis ordered the Jewish police to appear in full uniform beside the station in order to "prepare for air attacks". 140 policemen appeared as demanded; immediately armed German soldiers forced them to enter vehicles, and drove them to the Ninth Fort. There they were severely tortured; it was demanded that they reveal the location and hiding places of the underground movement. Only seven policemen out of the 140 broke under torture and were willing to reveal these locations. All the other police officers never disclosed any information. The Nazis murdered thirty-six of these policemen including: the chief of police and his assistants. Surprisingly, the remainder of these officers was returned to the ghetto.

Chapter Ten:

On September 15, 1943, the "quiet" period in the ghetto ended. The SS assumed control of the ghetto by taking control away from the German civil authorities and converting the ghetto into the Kauen Concentration Camp also known as Kovno Concentration Camp. This increased the German control over the Jews' daily lives and decreased the Jewish Council's role also known as "The Altestenrat". As winter was quickly approaching another two thousand Jewish laborers were forced to move out of Kovno Concentration Camp and into smaller labor camps throughout Lithuania, Latvia and Estonia. These labor camps were like the German Concentration Camps: men were separated from women and forbidden to meet; they dressed in "striped pajamas" and there were forced to stand for two roll calls daily: morning and evening.

Slowly, Naftali's' family members started disappearing from the ghetto, never to be seen from again. Naftali's Aunt on his mother's side, Rachol was married and had 2 daughters, one day the Germans separated a portion of the Ghetto where they were living and took all the residents to a forest in Riga where they were all shot to death. Rochol, her husband and both daughters were all killed in the forest in Riga. Naftali's uncle on his mother's side, Chaim Back was married with 3 sons when one day the entire family vanished. All were presumed dead: shot in the Ninth Fort. Another one of Naftali's uncles on his mother's side, Uncle Issac Back and his wife had two sons and lived separately from the Grandmother. One of their sons, Froska, ran away to Russia, when the Germans were invading Lithuania and managed to survive the war in a camp in Siberia. The other son, Bobka remained in the ghetto with his father and worked as a printer with his father and Naftali's father.

Naftali's Aunt Chaya on his father's side was married to Fishel and they had 4 children, 2 daughters, Hannah and Esther, and 2 sons, Yenkel and Chaimley. On October 26, 1943, the Nazis divided the ghetto and two thousand eight hundred men, women, and children were removed from the ghetto by force and with much cruelty, and were sent to Concentration Camps in Estonia to work in the forest. Aunt Chaya with Uncle Fishel and their four children were all forced to leave Kovno Concentration Camp. Their family was separated; the women were sent to one Concentration Camp in Estonia while the men were sent to another concentration camp in Estonia. Hannah and Esther's mother became ill while in the camp and did not survive, both brothers also perished while in the concentration camps. Hannah and Esther reunited with their father once they were transported to Stutthof Concentration Camp and that is where they learned that their brothers did not survive. They were not reunited for long, as Hannah and Esther were sent to work in an ammunition factory. Hannah was taught how to repair these special machines and

Esther worked producing ammunition. They were not allowed to leave and they remained in this factory day and night for months. They were both eventually transported to Bergen Belsen Concentration Camp. Unfortunately, their father did not survive the war and perished in the camps.

It felt like every other day the Germans would cut off sections from the ghetto, deporting Jews and making the ghetto smaller and smaller. Naftali and his family were able to remain in their Grandmother's house at 42 Aregelos street until May 1, 1942. On that date their home near the fence was annexed from the ghetto and they were forced to move. They found a place to live at 28 Varniu Street, which was in close proximity to "The Altestenrat". Naftali's family and Grandmother moved into this house with his Aunt Mena with her two daughters, and his Aunt Tsila with her daughter. They remained in this home until the ghetto was liquated in July 1944.

Naftali's Aunt Chaya on his mother's side was forced to move out from his grandmother's house and out of the ghetto with her husband, Shmuel and son, David and his wife, Shandel with her mother to a labor camp near the forest to chop wood to produce energy; they would burn the wood to make steam to propel the trains instead of gasoline. Chaya and Shmuel had another son, Yankel Koton but the Lithuanians murdered him when the Germans defeated the Russians in June of 1941. Naftali's Uncle Motel from his father's side with his wife Luba and their two daughters were also forced to move out from the Grandmother's house but they were forced to move to Alexod, which is a satellite labor camp in the suburb of Aleksotas, near the military airport. The Nazis moved the laborers closer to the airfields to continue to work on expanding and repairing the military airport. The Nazis stopped sending the Jews from Kovno Concentration Camp on a daily basis to the airport; rather they just kept the slave laborers in the camp near the airport on a permanent basis.

From September 1943 until July 1944, the Nazis managed to disperse more than 3,500 Jews from Kovno Concentration Camp to sub camps where strict discipline and abuse ruled all aspects of daily life. On March 27, 1944, the Nazis deported another 250 children and remaining elderly to Auschwitz Concentration Camp where they were all gassed upon arrival. Seven to eight thousand Jews were now left in Kovno Concentration Camp and they were forced to live in a tiny area.

The Jews inside the Concentration Camp realized their time was quickly coming to an end as they heard the news; the Soviet Army was approaching Lithuania since the Germans had been defeated at the front. They knew the Nazis would never allow them to live therefore the Jewish people desperately started searching for ways to save themselves. Either through hiding inside the ghetto, escaping from the ghetto and trying to find a place to hide in the city of Kovno or running away to the forest and joining the resistance underground.

The Ninth Fort continued to be the primary location for mass executions by the Nazis but now with the Russians approaching they needed to erase the evidence of their crimes. Soviet prisoners of war and Jews were forced to exhume the tens of thousands of bodies and burn them. These prisoners were all held at the Ninth Fort and they were fully aware that once they finished the job of erasing the past, they would be shot and killed. On December 25, 1943, 64 prisoners managed to escape through a tunnel in the Fort's cellar while the Nazis were celebrating Christmas. Thirteen of the escapees hid in Kovno and documented the German efforts to destroy the evidence of mass killings at the Ninth Fort.

Chapter Eleven:

On July 2, 1944 the Nazis sent their final decree. Kovno Concentration Camp was to be liquated and all the remaining inmates were to be evacuated to Germany. Everyone was to pack up their belongings in one suitcase and present themselves at the Concentration Camp gates. The Russian Army was so close to liberating Kovno that the Jewish people believed if they could hide, then they could be saved. This was a terrifying time and on July 8, 1944, Naftali's family decided to go into hiding along with two thousand other Jewish inmates. Naftali's brother, Meier decided to hide with his wife Bella and her family in their attic. Naftali's family then decided to hide with Bella and her family. After a few hours, the German's starting patrolling the streets and shouting that all printers need to come out and return to work. Naftali's father believed it was safer to leave their hiding place and go back to work. Meier wanted to stay with his wife, Bella and her family. Zalman insisted that Meier leave with his family. Meier agreed to leave and Bella joined them. Bella's parents, brother and sister remained hidden in the attic of their home.

When Naftali's family left their hiding place, the Nazis instructed them all to go to the Jewish Community Center. Upon arrival, Naftali's father Zalman, Naftali's Uncle Issac Back and Naftali's cousin Chaim Selsky were printers and the Nazis took them all away to the printing factory in the city of Kovno. The printers never returned. Chaim Selsky, Naftali's cousin managed to escape the printing factory and survived in the forest until the Russians liberated Kovno. Chaim Selsky then traveled to the Displaced Person's camp in Germany, at the end of the war and found Naftali and Meier. That was when they discovered that all the printers were shot dead inside the printing factory, including their father Zalman. Such devastating news!! Zalman worked so hard to save his entire family and then so close to liberation was executed.

The remaining family left behind in the Jewish Community Center locker rooms included Naftali, his Grandmother Ite Rive, his mother Rosa, his sister Zipora, his brother Meier with his wife Bella, Naftali's Aunt Tsila with her daughter, his Aunt Mena with her two daughters, his Uncle Motel with his wife Luba and their two daughters, his cousin Bobka Back (his father was Issac Back - one of the printers taken away with Zalman and Chaim) with his Mother and Uncle Shmuel Koton with his wife Chaya and their son David Koton. They were held in the locker room for a day and a half without food or water. They were then instructed to march to the train station. They were surrounded on both sides with armed German and Lithuanian guards; there was no opportunity to escape. They were all shoved onto cattle trains, men, women and children with two buckets, one with water and the other for waste. When they sealed the boxcar there was no air in the car, no windows, no food and they were crammed altogether like animals.

On July 8, 1944 the Germans and Lithuanians, began the five-day process of setting fire to the former ghetto, to force the Jews out of their hiding places. The SS ordered the German troops to blow up every house, as they were suspicious that the Jews might be hiding in underground bunkers. The Germans used smoke grenades, firebombs, dynamite and bloodhounds to force the Jews out into the open. The Germans were throwing grenades over potential hiding places and the houses burned down over these hiding places, trapping the victims under all the debris. When they finished blowing up each individual house, they then poured gasoline over what was left of the ghetto and incinerated it: to destroy any evidence of their crime. Only one bunker was able to survive the bombings and the fires. Approximately twenty-one people including a Rabbi survived for nearly a month in a bunker underneath the fires. They only came out of their hiding place once they heard their mother tongue being spoken overhead. The Germans were finally GONE!!! Only a total of 500 Jewish people managed to survive in the forests and in the one remaining bunker. Meier's wife, Bella lost her mother, father, brother and sister in the burning of the Kovno Ghetto. They perished in their attic-hiding place.

Three weeks later, on August 1, 1944, the Soviet army arrived in Kovno to liberate the camp, but it was already too late for most of the Jews of the Kovno Ghetto. The Germans had already destroyed the ghetto to the ground with grenades and dynamite. As many as two thousand more people had burned to death, been buried alive or had been shot while trying to escape, while the remaining Jewish population of the Kovno Ghetto were already dead or were on their way to Hitler's extermination camps.

Of the original forty thousand Jews in the Kovno Ghetto, only approximately three thousand of them survived. By the end of the War (April 1945), 95% of the total Jewish population of Lithuania had fallen victim to Hitler's "Final Solution". Only eight thousand to nine thousand Lithuanian Jews remained alive from the prewar population of two hundred thirty five thousand.

Chapter Twelve:

From July 8, 1944 until July 13, 1944, the Germans emptied the camp, transporting the remaining Jews in cattle cars first to Stutthof Concentration Camp, near Danzig on the Baltic Coast and then on to Dachau Concentration Camp in Germany. Stutthof was established in September 1939, which was built in the wooded area of west Stutthof, which is in Poland. Stutthof was the first camp the Germans built outside of Germany. In November 1941, the camp became a labor camp, and then in January 1942, Stutthof became a regular concentration camp. Barbed-wire fences guarded the entire old camp and when the camp was enlarged, electric barbed-wire fences surrounded the camp. In 1943, the Nazis added a crematory and a gas chamber. The gas chamber was only able to hold a maximum of 150 people at one time. When the SS had too many people to execute, they also used vans as gas chambers. The SS soldiers sent the prisoners that were too weak or sick to work to the gas chambers. The doctors of the camps also killed the sick and injured prisoners in the infirmary by using lethal injections. In June 1944, Stutthof became a major part of the final solution and a mass extermination camp.

Within five years of its creation, Stutthof grew from a small camp intended for 3,500 prisoners (in 1940) to a complex of 39 sub camps that held 110,000 people from 25 countries. Among the prisoners were Poles, Jews, Russians, Ukrainians, Lithuanians, Latvians, Estonians, Czechs, Slovaks, Finns, Norwegians, French, Danes, Dutch, Germans, Austrians, English, Spanish, Italians, Yugoslavs, Hungarians, and Gypsies. Prisoners were exposed to slave labor, malnutrition, terrible sanitation, disease, and mental and physical torture. An estimated 65,000 people died as a result of the living conditions, as well as executions by shooting, hanging, gassing, lethal injection, beatings and torture.

A man named Rudolf Spanner, an SS officer and "scientist", was the creator and owner of the small soap factory located in Danzig. In 1940, he invented the process to produce soap from human fat. The product he created was called "Reines Judische Fett" (R.J.S.). This means "Pure Jewish Fat" and many Jewish prisoners were executed to produce soap. Rudolf was very, very proud of his "invention." The allies discovered chambers full of corpses used for the production of soap. After the war was over, Rudolf was never arrested and continued his "research" for his horrible invention.

Naftali and his remaining family were crammed together for hours until the train arrived to Stutthof Concentration Camp. The SS opened the car doors to all the boxcars and with their barking dogs ordered all the women and children off the train. Naftali's brother Meier tried to get his wife Bella to put on a pair of men's pants to pretend she was a man so she would stay with them on the train. Uncle

Shmuel Koton screamed at Meier " NO, you will get us all killed!!" Bella got off the train and Meier got off the train with her. The Germans immediately stopped him and forced him back on the train.

The doors to the cattle car were sealed once again and the men were trapped with no food, no air and no room as they left Stutthof Concentration Camp without the women and children of their family. It was too much to bear not knowing what would happen to their loved ones. Upon arriving at the train station the women and children were forced to line up and a selection took place where the young and fit women were sent to live while the children and older women were sent to the gas chambers. Bella watched as Naftali's mother, Rosa was sent to live while her daughter Zipora (since she was short for her age) was sent to death. Rosa decided life was not worth living without her family and would not leave her daughter alone. She walked over to the other side to be with her daughter, which meant death. That was the last time Bella saw Rosa and Tzipora. It was also the last time she saw Naftali's Grandmother Ite Rive, Aunt Tsila and her daughter, Aunt Mena and her two daughters, Uncle Motel's wife, Luba, and Uncle Shmuel's wife Chaya Koton. They were all sent to the gas chambers.

Bella was sent to the labor camp with Uncle Motel's two daughters, Hanetkeh and Munka and with Uncle Shmuel's son's wife Shandel Koton with her mother. Bella, Shandel and her mother were the only female members of Naftali's family that survived Stutthof Concentration Camp. Hanetkeh and Munka survived the hardship of the labor camp until the bitter end when they were forced on a death march to escape the oncoming allies. After marching for days Hanetkeh was ordered to carry some food for an SS guard. When she was handing the food back to the guard, he shot her. Her sister Munka, ran to her aide and he shot and killed her too. They were only hours away from freedom!

The remaining men left alive in Naftali's family were Naftali, his brother Meier, Uncle Shmuel Koton and his son David Koton, Bobka Back, son of Uncle Issac Back and Uncle Motel Schlomowitz. These men continued on their journey to Dachau, which took two to three days; they were treated like animals trapped and packed into cattle cars, under horrible conditions, without any food or water and sanitary facilities. The train arrived outside of Dachau Concentration Camp in Landsberg. They were pushed off the trains and forced to walk to Lager I, this was the sub-camp for Dachau; also known as the working camp. In the summer and fall of 1944, to increase war production, Dachau prisoners built sub-camps near weapon factories throughout southern Germany and all these sub-camps were under the administration of Dachau. These sub-camps housed able-bodied prisoners who were used as slave labor to manufacture weapons and other materials for Germany's efforts in World War II. Forced labor using concentration camp prisoners became more and more important to German's weapon production. Dachau had more than 30 large sub-camps in which over 30,000 prisoners worked almost exclusively on armaments. Thousands of prisoners were worked to death.

They were forced to remove all their clothes while the Nazis took them away and handed them clothing that looked like pajamas, striped grey/blue jacket, pants and a rain poncho. They also took away their shoes and gave them wooden shoes called "clumpus". The shoes were broken down into two parts where the front part was attached to the back half with leather. These shoes were wooden clogs with no shoelaces; they just needed to slip their feet into these hard wooden clogs without socks. The Germans handed every prisoner a metal soup bowl with a handle and a cover. That was their only utensil during their entire stay in Dachau.

The Nazis also took away any jewelry, money and all personal possessions they might have been able to hide in the ghetto and smuggle with them into the camp. While Naftali and his family were forced to stand in rows in the center of Lager I, the Germans chose three to four prisoners to go to the toilets to search for jewelry that were thrown inside the latrine in order to avoid handing them over to the Germans. These toilets were in an outhouse with one long piece of wood, like a bench with holes drilled in it for seats. These poor men needed to drop inside the latrine, under the wood and search through the manure for jewelry, which they did manage to find. The one item Naftali managed to hide from the Germans was a family photo of himself before the war with his mother, father, sister and brother. He hid this photo inside his wooden shoe. Naftali managed to save this photo throughout his time in Dachau and this remains the only photo he has of his mother, father and sister. (see photo in the back of the book)

The evacuation of the prisoners in Stutthof camp occurred in January 1945. 50,000 prisoners were evacuated from the camp and 5,000 of them were forced to march to the Baltic Sea. From there they were forced into the water and machine-gunned. The rest of the prisoners were forced to march in the direction of Landsburg, eastern Germany. The prisoners were rescued by Soviet forces. Sadly, many died during the march and they were so close to being saved by the Soviets. Over 25,000 prisoners, one in two, died during the evacuation from Stutthof Concentration Camp and over 65,000 prisoners were killed in the camp. On May 9, 1945, the Soviet forces liberated Stutthof Camp and also found and liberated 100 prisoners that managed to hide during the final evacuation. Stutthof was the last camp to be liberated by the allies.

Chapter Thirteen:

After standing in rows for hours, Naftali with his family members, were assigned to tents. They had to sleep on the bare ground with only straw for mattresses. Eventually they were moved into barracks. The stench from the barracks hit them before they even stepped inside. The smell of death mixed with disease, starvation and humiliation filled the air. The barrack was built to hold about a hundred people; it was filled with over one thousand eight hundred prisoners. These barracks were filled with members of any group considered by Hitler to not be of the Aryan, perfect race. Among them were artists, intellectuals and other independent thinkers; Communists, Jehovah's Witnesses and others who were opposed to the Nazi Party; Homosexuals and others who were viewed as sexually deviant; Gypsies and Catholic Clergy and of course the Jews. The physically and mentally handicapped were sent to Dachau earlier on in the war but were killed by exposure to lethal gas in the gas chambers and then burned in the crematorium when these buildings were built in Dachau in 1942. The barracks were rows upon rows of wooden planks built one on top of another like bunk beds to hold more people. There were no pillows, sheets or padding for these wooden boards. They had to sleep ten to a section, one next to the other and they slept in their striped bottoms, jacket, and poncho with their shoes on. Everybody was given one blanket. Meier was not assigned to the same barrack as Naftali. The SS would wake them up at 4am to stand still in roll call for hours. They needed to do this again at night after working all day. Some men would fall in their place from exhaustion and starvation and would then be shot dead.

Dachau prisoners were used as forced laborers. At first, they were employed in the operation of the camp, in various construction projects. Prisoners built roads, worked in gravel pits, and drained marshes. Initially Naftali's jobs changed daily. First he was sent to move railroad tracks from one location to another. These tracks were incredibly heavy and this work was back breaking. Another day, Naftali was sent to load 50-pound bags of cement onto trucks, these bags were also unbelievably heavy and this job was just as back breaking.

On yet another day, Naftali was sent on an 8-10 kilometers march into the forest where there was a factory being built, hidden from site, deep inside the forest. It was a very long factory and from the outside it looked like a very high cave. This factory was built to work and store airplane parts and it was hidden in the forest to be protected from bombings from the German's enemies. Naftali with the rest of the prisoners were there to build the factory's roof. It was made with iron and cement; made to withstand any bombings. First Naftali needed to unload trains filled with 50-pound bags of cement. He then needed to pour the cement powder through a mesh filter and add water from another pipe into mixers- the dust was unbearable. Naftali would choke and cough all day long. Then Naftali had to bend the iron into all types of shapes and fill the iron with cement to equal 6 meters in thickness to build the exterior roof. He vividly remembers holding a one-inch thick iron bar that was 9 meters in length with his bare hands and in order to bend this bar he needed to run in a circle with this iron bar while the Germans fed the other end of the bar into a machine. It was pouring rain and Naftali was getting soaked and he kept suffering from electric shocks since he was holding onto this iron bar in this rainstorm with thunder and lightening. The German guard allowed Naftali to stop by the fire to try to dry off his jacket but then he needed to return to the same job and became soaked once again. When his day was finally finished and he returned to his barrack, he slept in his wet clothes, as he had no other clothes to change into.

Naftali became terribly sick and developed a horrible fever; he was unable to even eat the ration of a slice of bread a day. He became very weak but continued to work. There was a doctor in this camp and Naftali was told to go the barrack where all the sick people were held. When Naftali went over to this barrack, he saw sick people lying everywhere with huge insects such as lice walking all over them and eating them alive. Naftali refused to stay in these barracks so he returned to his barrack and continued to work. His brother Meier was very concerned for his brother, he decided to save his dark bread rations and after several days traded in his rations for a slice of white bread. Meier hoped that Naftali would be able to eat and digest the white bread; he hoped it would be easier on his digestive system. Unfortunately, Naftali was still not able to eat the white bread.

One day upon returning from work in the middle of winter, Naftali and his barrack inmates were ordered to go directly to the showers. All the prisoners were terrified that they were being sent to the gas chambers. When they approached the showers they were relieved to see a window was open; this meant that there was no gas and they were really going for a shower. Naftali still had a high fever and with the windows open and since no towels were provided: he became sicker. The doctor diagnosed him with double pneumonia. Naftali finally went to the barrack for sick people and he stayed there for several weeks. He remembers one day the Red Cross delivered packages to the ill. These packages contained cigarettes, chocolate and one can of condensed sweet milk. The milk was like heaven and was very nourishing. The man lying next to Naftali was very ill and he traded his food for cigarettes with anyone that would trade. Naftali traded his cigarettes for this man's food. This man never ate anything; he owed his food to everyone so he could smoke. He eventually passed away.

Naftali was re-assigned to work in the kitchen, as he was still very sick, even after spending several weeks in the sick barracks. Meier was already working in the kitchen. They would cook big pots of soup for the German guards. They would mix soup with vegetables and would mash peas, cornflakes and oatmeal to the soup to thicken it up. Occasionally a big chunk of oatmeal would float to the top of the soup and Naftali would scoop it out with his container/bowl, which he kept on him at all times. He then hid the oatmeal in his poncho and when he returned to his barrack he would share the piece of oatmeal with his brother, Meier.

One day when Meier was working in the kitchen, his Uncle Motel came to see him. Motel was Meier's father's brother and was placed in Lager II, which was another sub camp of Dachau Concentration Camp. They would occasionally see each other whenever the prisoners from Lager II would be allowed to go the kitchen in Lager I. This time when Uncle Motel found Meier he told him he could no longer go on. He found life in the concentration camp unbearable and he lost the will to survive. He did not see an end to the war and was unable to sustain himself any longer just for the hope that one-day the Nazis would be defeated and brought to justice. It seemed like that day would never arrive. The prisoners in the camps had no access to newspapers or radios, they had no idea if the Germans were winning or losing the war. They had no idea if their time in the camps was coming to an end or not. The Nazis made sure that the prisoners were kept in the dark. If the prisoners had any hope that the war was coming to an end, the Nazis feared that the prisoners would rebel. The time in Lager II-Dachau Concentration Camp was torturous for Motel and he came to say good-bye to Meier and to tell Naftali, he sends his love and to tell him he says good-bye as well. As hard as Meier tried to change his mind, nothing helped. Uncle Motel's mind was made up, his decision was final and he was taking his life. This was devastating news for Naftali and Meier. Cousin Bobka

Back who was with them in Dachau already died from dysentery and now Uncle Motel. Their family was growing smaller and smaller and who knew how much longer the remaining family members would be able to survive.

Chapter Fourteen:

The daily food rations consisted of one piece of dark black bread, a cup of tea in the morning and a bowl of soup for dinner. At first, the soup was full of potatoes. As the war progressed, the soup no longer had any potatoes; it was just broth and primarily water. The Germans hid the potatoes in a basement cellar. Since the men were starving, any opportunity to steal food was considered, even if the punishment meant death. Naftali saw an opportunity and grabbed it but first he needed to fabricate a way to get a hold of those potatoes. In their bathroom, the sink was one big trough where many people could wash their hands at once. Naftali managed to break off a long piece of wood from under the sink and was able to stick a nail at the end of the bar. At night, Naftali would sneak out of his barracks and walk along the shadows in the camp. He came upon the cellar where the potatoes were being stored. There was a small window way above the location of the potatoes. Naftali would lie on his stomach and use the wooden bar to poke at the potatoes with the nail in an attempt to catch a potato. Naftali was extremely patient since he had no trouble catching a potato but once it was being lifted out, it would hit the screen and fall to the ground. He still managed to catch and smuggle 2 potatoes every time he went.

One night, while he was lying in the dark outside the cellar window, he heard a noise and thought...this is it, I am getting caught stealing potatoes and they will hang me for this. With much relief, it was a fellow prisoner with the same idea to steal potatoes. After smuggling the potatoes back to the barrack, Naftali would hide the potatoes in the bathroom ceiling. He would slide the ceiling tiles over and hide the potatoes on the beams in the ceiling. He would then go wake up his brother, Meier and tell him where he hid the potatoes. The next day, Meier would take the potatoes and bring them to work with him as Meier was working a different shift than Naftali and was able to cook the potatoes over a fire. When Meier would return to the barracks after work, he would put Naftali's potato all cooked back in the same hiding spot. Naftali managed to steal potatoes about twice a week.

One morning, when Naftali was going to the kitchen to get his cup of tea, he saw a pot of soup was left on the stove. He quickly managed to lift the lid on the pot of soup and used his bowl that he carried with him to scoop out a bowl of soup. The next day, Naftali tried the same thing but this time things did not go as planned. All the prisoners noticed Naftali scooping out soup and ran towards him to try and get soup for themselves. It made quite a scene and the German Kapos came running. Naftali was the last man left at the scene because everybody else ran away. The German Kapo beat Naftali over his head with a piece of wood. This beating was excruciatingly painful for days upon days. Since this beating, Naftali has suffered from severe migraines and headaches for his entire life.

Everyday, all the concentration camp inmates needed to stand for hours upon hours for roll call. Naftali stated that the Nazis would constantly select those prisoners they considered unfit for work and thus were doomed to die. One day, there was a large selection. The German guards removed one hundred and twenty boys that they deemed unfit to live and were sent to Aushwitz Concentration Camp also known as the death camp. The only thing they could see that was wrong with these boys was that they were short. Therefore Naftali and his brother Meier would stand on their tiptoes during this selection process and for all the future selections. Their camp uniforms were so long that it allowed them to stand up on their tiptoes and no one noticed. This act alone saved both their lives. Some of these boys survived Aushwitz and Naftali met up with them in the Displaced Person Camp after the war in

Germany and they told him where they were sent after the selection.

Naftali's cousin, David Koton broke his finger one day while performing his labor duties. He was re-assigned to serve the German "Elderstat". These men were German prisoners who were put in charge of the other prisoners. These men had their own small barracks and lived separately from the rest of the prisoners. They received special privileges such as more food and better clothing and better shoes. David Koton was responsible for maintaining their barracks, cleaning their shoes and clothes and whatever chores they wanted him to do for them. Occasionally when Naftali had some time off, like at the end of his workday, he would go and visit David. David would give him a big container of soup and Naftali would sneak it back to his barrack and share the soup with his brother, Meier and his uncle, Shmuel Koton (David's father). This extra soup helped sustain them and keep up their strength to continue to work in order to live. Anyone unfit to work would immediately be killed. Shmuel Koton's job was to maintain the washrooms and to keep the fire in the washroom fireplace lit at all times. This was not considered a very strenuous job and he was fortunate enough to have this job. He was assigned this job since he knew these two Jewish brothers, Schitock brothers who were responsible for kitchen duties and distribution of food. They were able to assign Shmuel Koton his job and therefore Shmuel Koton was able to survive Dachau Concentration Camp, Lager I.

Originally, Dachau Concentration Camp was only for men, there were no women for many years. One day, one woman appeared as her husband made her dress up like a man so they can remain together throughout the war. The German "Elderstat" discovered the woman hiding among the men and separated her from the men. He placed her in her own barrack and then three hundred additional women from Hungary and Czech Republic were brought into the camp to join her in this barrack. Everyone was forced to live under inhumane conditions. Amongst these woman was a mother and her son was held separately in the men's barracks.

One day, the Nazis hung four men. The Nazis made examples and hung inmates in public to intimidate the rest of the prisoners. One of these prisoners that was hung that day was the mother's son. She was forced to stand and watch like all the prisoners as her son was hung to death. The reason he was hung was unbelievable. The uniforms that the German's provided the prisoners included a jacket, a pair of pants, a poncho, a pair of wooden clog shoes and a blanket. They were not given socks. This man was cold and decided to cut up his blanket to make himself some socks. The Germans discovered that he cut his blanket and hung him for this. How horrific and to have his mother watch his execution is beyond words!

Chapter Fifteen:

From time to time, Naftali and his fellow prisoners would hear airplanes flying overhead. The German guards would make them all lie down on the ground. These planes were not German warplanes but rather American and Russian fighter planes, but they never dropped any bombs on the concentration camp. As much as they prayed that they would just drop a bomb to stop their torture, it never happened. These planes would fly low to the ground and appeared to get a good view of the entire concentration camp, maybe even taking pictures but nothing else; much to everyone's disappointment.

Slowly, slowly prisoners started arriving from other concentration camps as their camps were closing. These prisoners arrived by death marches and on trains. If it is at all possible to even consider, these prisoners looked in worse shape than the prisoners from Dachau Concentration Camp. These men looked like the walking dead, they were only skin and bones. There is a name for these men, "Muselmann". They would arrive day and night freezing cold with frostbitten toes and fingers as their clothes were made from rags, their shoes were made of wood with no socks or boots and clearly not appropriately dressed for the cold German winters, just like the prisoners in Dachau. They would be starving, as they were never given any food or water during their days of marching or days on the trains. Dachau Concentration Camp was the last camp to close, as it was deep in Germany; Munich, Germany and prisoners were coming from all over German-Occupied Europe.

The death marches started in their labor camp, Lager I, on April 25, 1945. The German guards would round up several hundred prisoners and remove them from their camp and start them on a death march to the main camp, Dachau Concentration Camp that was 40 kilometers away. The main camp had the gas chambers and crematoriums and this was the way the Nazis could kill any remaining survivors so there were no witnesses left alive. Of course, the Germans were telling everyone that they were being relocated to Terol, Switzerland to exchange the prisoners from Dachau for German prisoners.

Naftali did not believe the lies that the Germans were telling them all. He tried desperately to avoid going on any of the marches. He would stand in a line for hours while the chief camp doctor, who was Jewish was forced to select the prisoners for the death marches. Initially, the camp doctor selected the stronger prisoners who he thought would survive the 40-kilometer march. This took days upon days. Naftali spoke with the doctor and explained that he was with his brother Meier and he was just released from the camp hospital and is still very weak. The doctor was kind and understanding and did not choose Naftali or Meier to go on any of these marches.

After the selections were finished for the day, Naftali and his brother, Meier went to David

Koton's barrack. David Koton was staying in the "Elderstat" barrack because as mentioned earlier he was assigned to clean this barrack of the German prisoners who was in charge of the other prisoners. These German prisoners were political prisoners so they received extra privileges with extra food rations. The "Elderstat" lived in the same barracks with the "Lager Elster". The "Lager Elster" was also a political German prisoner but his responsibility was to document all the reports for each and everyday in the camp. David Koton was also responsible for the day-to-day life of both the "Elderstat" and the "Lager Elster". During the liquidation of the concentration camp the Germans were searching for the "Lager Elster". They wanted to kill him because he knew too much. Meier, Naftali and David Koton saw the "Lager Elster" go into hiding. He was not a bad man and they hoped he would not be captured.

In the meantime, Naftali, Meier, Shmuel and David all stayed in the "Elderstat" barracks for an entire day: hiding. They had no food or water but they decided it was not safe to leave the barracks for fear of being captured and sent on a death march. Eventually, the Germans stopped any food distribution throughout the camps. Naftali thought it would be safe for him to return to his barracks, as he wanted to get his knapsack. Upon returning to David Koton's barrack, he noticed the German guards were grabbing prisoners and putting them in lines for yet another death march. This time Naftali was captured by a German guard and thrown in line with the other prisoners. Naftali was devastated that he was caught and decided when the opportunity would present itself he would escape, even if it meant death.

As they were all forced to start marching, Naftali found an opportunity to escape. The German guard, who grabbed him, turned his head for a split second and Naftali managed to run to the toilets, which were outhouses. He managed to jump the wall behind the toilets where there were more toilets and he ran through the back door and continued running in between the barracks. He did not stop running until he returned to David Koton's barrack. It was very foolish of him to leave the barrack in the first place and he was lucky he managed to escape and was not shot in the process.

By the next day, in the afternoon, Meier, Naftali, Shmuel and David decided to go in search of food. They noticed an empty truck pull into the camp and it drove to the kitchen. They followed the truck and saw that the Germans were loading the truck with loaves of bread, all that was left in the kitchen. Naftali managed to grab a couple of loaves of bread but before he could even take one-step away from the truck he was attacked from all sides. The prisoners who arrived by death marches; the "Muselmann" who were just skin, bones and two deep sockets for eyes, pounced on top of Naftali. Naftali tried in vain to hide the loaves of bread inside his poncho but the men were all on top of him, grabbing pieces of the bread and scratching him with their nails. The weight of all these men on top of Naftali became unbearable and slowly, slowly Naftali was unable to breath. There were at least 6 men on top of him and Naftali was completely helpless under all these men. Then Meier, his brother began picking up the men, one by one, off of Naftali. Another minute and Naftali would have been buried alive under the weight of these men, all for a couple of loaves of bread.

Naftali managed to save a few loaves of bread from under his poncho and gave one loaf to Meier and kept one loaf for himself. They hid the loaves of bread in their knapsack. They kept this knapsack with them throughout their year in Dachau's Lager I Concentration Camp. They decided not to eat their bread even though they had not had any food in days but they thought that they should save the bread because who knows what tomorrow will hold. Who could imagine anything worse then what they had survived but living through their hell they knew that things could be worse and they better be prepared.

Chapter Sixteen:

Another truck arrived into the camp and it was also empty. This time the German guards were selecting prisoners to put on the trucks to bring them to the train stations. This was instead of the death marches. Naftali, Meier, David and Shmuel Koton decided they wanted to climb on board this truck to avoid being forced into a death march. They believed it would no longer be safe to remain in the camp, as they feared the Germans would burn down the camp to destroy any proof or evidence of this camp: just like they burned down Kovno Ghetto. The guards selected David and his father, Shmuel Koton to board the truck but unfortunately Naftali and Meier were not selected. The truck drove away with their only remaining family members while Naftali and Meier were left behind to watch and pray that one day they would be reunited.

Later that day another truck drove into the camp and once again the German guards were selecting the prisoners who were allowed to board the truck. One man jumped onto the truck without permission and the German guard shot him dead. He was left hanging from the truck for everyone to see and fear. This was the way the Germans played with the prisoners' minds. It was another ghastly site just like witnessing the hanging of the innocent prisoners. The German officer was running around the truck making sure no one else would jump onto the truck without permission and while he was on one side of the truck, Naftali and Meier jumped into the truck. Luckily they were not caught and they managed to stay on the truck: alive.

Eventually the truck was filled to capacity and it left Lager I- Labor Camp/Concentration Camp for the train station in the town of Landsberg, Germany. This town was approximately 3-4 kilometers away from Lager I. Once the truck arrived to the train station all the prisoners were forced off the truck and ordered to load up onto yet another train. Unbeknown to Naftali or Meier, David and Shmuel Koton were on the same train as them but in another car. This time, the train had benches, this was the first time that the train was not a boxcar meant to transport cattle but rather was a passenger train with benches and windows. They were forced to stay on this train until early morning and once again no food or water was ever distributed. As the trains were moving through the forest in the direction of Dachau Concentration Camp where they had the gas chambers and crematoriums, Naftali heard planes flying overhead. These planes began firing on the train. Naftali and the other prisoners on the train all climbed under the bench in an effort to protect themselves while the train came to a complete stop.

After a few minutes, the gunfire stopped and Naftali fearfully and with lots of hesitation looked out the window. The cars in front of Naftali's car were filled with Russian prisoners from the German Air Force. Most of them were injured or killed because their cars were in close proximity to the engine and that was where the planes were firing. The planes were American warplanes with American fighter pilots who were shooting at the trains, in an attempt to stop them from arriving to their destination, the extermination camp in the main camp of Dachau. The German guards were all in the front of the train, which was where the engine was. Unfortunately, the guards were not injured but these guards feared for their own lives and disconnected their engine car from the remainder of the train and left the scene.

Naftali along with the other prisoners were slowly getting up from the floor as the firing had stopped and the planes were gone. When Naftali looked out the window he saw German guards who did not escape with the other guards. These guards were taking off their German uniforms and putting on overalls from the German Air Force. They were actually removing the uniforms from the dead prisoners so that when the allies arrived they would think they were prisoners and not German guards. These guards then ran into the forest to escape. It was unbelievable to think that these monsters were getting away with their crimes and would never be captured or punished in a court of law. This was too much to consider at this time because they were now worried about surviving themselves.

As the German guards were not returning, Naftali and his brother, Meier, took advantage of the opportunity and broke open their train door. They then ran to all the cars and pried open all the doors to free all the prisoners. One of the cars was filled with the loaves of bread that the Germans took from the kitchen in Lager I. Naftali and Meier were able to grab a few more loaves of bread, and then they ran away into the forest. All the prisoners started running into the forest to escape. As they were all exhausted and starving, all the prisoners just started to lie down to go to sleep. When Naftali and Meier awoke they discovered that their loaves of bread were gone.

Someone had stolen Naftali's bread from his knapsack and since they were unable to open Meier's knapsack they ripped open Meier's knapsack to steal his bread and destroyed his knapsack. They were very upset, as they should have eaten their bread when they had it instead of saving it. Naftali decided to risk his life to return to the train in order to steal more loaves of bread.

Before nightfall, the German guards returned to the train. These guards started shouting into the forest for everyone to come back to the train. Only a few prisoners returned while the remainder of the prisoners who were sleeping began to run away again. The Germans then started shooting into the forest, killing many prisoners who were attempting to escape. Naftali and Meier managed to run far enough away and then when they saw other prisoners they pretended to call them back to the trains so the Germans thought they were helping them. They noticed that there were German guards throughout the forest coming from all directions, shooting at any prisoner who was running or moving. They heard shots deep inside the forest and realized that those prisoners that did not rest while everyone else was sleeping tried to run deeper into the forest were now being captured and killed.

During the chaos of escaping Naftali and Meier came across two other men who they knew from the ghetto, Uri Chenoch and Utkah Lefshitz. They all managed to escape together by running further into the fields. They then decided to turn around and cross the train tracks far behind the train to fool the German guards. The Germans were hunting for the prisoners in the fields closest to the open doors of the train, when Naftali, Meier, Utkah and Uri crossed over the tracks they were able to escape into a much deeper forest without being noticed.

While they ran into the forest, they came across German soldiers who were wearing the German Air Force overalls and were pretending to be

Russian prisoners of war. They were able to easily recognize that these men were not prisoners but rather well fed German guards but these guards said "hello" and continued on their way. The guards chose to allow all four men in prison uniforms to continue on their way so they chose to allow the Germans to go on their way. It was still much too risky to cause any trouble as the German guards were still searching for prisoners to capture and send to the gas chambers. Understanding the war was nearing its end; their only thoughts were on escaping and surviving.

Chapter Seventeen:

Complete and utter exhaustion from running all day long and complete darkness were the only reasons that Naftali, Meier, Uri and Utkah stopped running. They came across some men yelling at them to come closer but they did not want to go. Meier finally decided to walk over to find out what the men wanted. They were Russian prisoners and wanted food. Meier gave them some bread and then returned to Naftali. The Russian prisoners wanted Meier to stay with them because Meier had some food but Meier refused. They decided to walk deeper into the field to find a good spot to rest. They noticed a fire at a distance but Naftali refused to approach the fire for fear it was much too dangerous. They all decided to stay together and they took turns sleeping. Three men would sleep for two hour shifts and the forth man would stay awake to watch. They took turns all night long to stay safe and alive.

In the morning, they started walking again deeper into the forest and came across a small observation tower with a booth at the top. It looked like an observation tower for airplanes. They all climbed up the tower hoping to find food. The only thing they found were bullets for a rifle but no rifle was found and no food was found either. From the top of the tower they noticed a large house in the distance. They were certainly nervous about approaching the house for fear of who would be in the house. Once again, Meier went alone to check out the house. Meier came across a Russian prisoner from the German Air Force; he was one of the prisoners who escaped from the German Air Force train the day before. He was also hiding inside the house. Meier called out for everyone to come into the house.

They decided to investigate the house and discovered that this house was the house for the German pilots. They found vodka, cans of beef and bread in the kitchen. They immediately sat down to start eating while the Russian prisoner joined them. They ate a very small amount of food: one small piece of bread, a bit of beef and a sip of vodka. Meier instructed everyone to eat only a small amount and then he ordered everyone to stop eating or they would be sick. The prisoners who received food from the allies died suddenly from the food they ate because their bodies could not tolerate it. They would eat too much food at once and their bodies would shut down. Untold thousands of survivors perished at liberation from the good deeds of their liberators who felt compelled to feed the starving prisoners.

Naftali and Meier continued to search the house and discovered rifles and bullets. They also discovered this house had a basement and much to their surprise this basement was filled with lots of various items: watches, jackets, pants, sheets, towels, suitcases, soap, cigars, cigarette lighters, typewriters, wheels of cheese and pails of meat. Items that no one had seen since before the war. Incredible to believe an entire basement right in the middle of a forest after 6 years of war filled with food, clothes and miscellaneous items. The men just stood there in the middle of this basement in complete and utter shock and disbelief. They then decided to prepare a place for all of them to sleep in a small room in the basement. Naftali then took one rifle and filled it with bullets to be prepared incase the Germans' returned to the house. Before they could go to sleep, they heard the Russian prisoner screaming for them to come out, that there was an American Soldier who wanted to see them. Meier once again said he would go first to investigate.

Meier returned after several minutes and told them all to come upstairs into the kitchen. It was ok, the American Soldier wanted to see them all and speak to them. They all went to meet the American Soldier in the kitchen where they also discovered more rooms with lockers. The soldier explained to them that now the American Soldiers will be staying in this house, it no longer belonged to the German soldiers and he asked them to stay in the house and be the cooks for the American Soldiers. They were welcomed to stay as long as they liked and they would be in charge of the kitchen. Luckily, Utkah knew how to cook and remembered how to cook. Naftali remembers helping Utkah prepare a delicious goulash. Not far from the house was a small German town by the name of "Petzenhausen". Naftali would ride his bicycle that he built, into town and buy some bread from the bakery. The four men stayed only 3 days in this house.

A new American Battalion of soldiers arrived on the third day and they were not so nice, unlike the first American Battalion. The officer from the second Battalion kicked out Meier, Naftali, Utkah and Uri. He stated they needed the rooms for their soldiers. Lucky once again, they were preparing to leave and Naftali was able to build four bicycles during the three days they were there, one for each of them. They also packed up bags filled with sheets, towels, soap, clothes such as pants and jackets and a pail of meat. Before they could leave the American officer from the second Battalion examined their belongings ensuring they did not take any weapons: rifles or bullets.

The four men then biked to the main town called Landsberg, Germany. When they arrived in Landsberg, they went directly to the Displaced Persons' Camp and asked the survivors if they knew David and Shmuel Koton and if they had seen them. Much to their good fortune, the survivors knew them and directed Naftali and Meier to them. It was a glorious reunion!! They discovered that David and Shmuel were on the same train as Naftali and Meier and also managed to escape into the fields and forest. Naftali and Meier then gave David and Shmuel the pail of meat and informed them that they had decided not to stay in Landsberg. They heard from other survivors that farmers in the town of Petzenhausen were helping the survivors recover with housing, rest and good food.

David, Shmuel, Uri and Utkah chose not to leave Landsberg but Meier and Naftali decided to leave on their own and headed to the farming community, in Petzenhausen, approximately 63 km away from Landsberg. Meier and Naftali traveled there on their bicycles and upon arrival they were greeted by another Jewish survivor who was in charge of assigning housing to the survivors. The American soldiers placed this Jewish man in charge of lodging assignments as well as assigning where the survivors would eat. Naftali and Meier moved in with a German farmer and his family; they had their own room with two beds on the second floor of the house. They slept in this one German family's house but would go for their three meals a day at another German family's house. It was approximately a five-minute walk to this farmer's house for meals but they could not stay there, as he did not have more available rooms for them. There were other Jewish men who were survivors from Dachau Concentration Camp that were living in this German farming community.

This small German farming community was very kind to the survivors in a time when they needed nourishment and kindness. Naftali and Meier stayed in this farming community for one month. They were well cared for, they received delicious food and a warm bed with a roof over their heads to allow them to heal and recover. The survivors, including Naftali and Meier never spoke of their experiences in the ghettos or camps, not amongst themselves and not to the German farmers and their families. This was a time for healing and moving forward and part of that was an attempt to move past their horrific experiences and look to the future. During their years in the ghettos and concentration camps there was no looking forward to the future, it did not look like they would survive to see a future but now under remarkable circumstances here they were trying to rebuild their strength so they can once again begin planning for their future.

Chapter Eighteen:

There came news from Landsberg that survivors were going back home in an attempt to reunite with their families, if any of their family members managed to survive!! Naftali and Meier decided they were now strong enough to travel and packed up their belongings and returned to Landsberg. Before leaving the farming community, they went around to say their good byes and to thank all the farmers for their kindness and generosity. Without their support, they would not have recovered as quickly as they did and they also gave them renewed faith in mankind, yes even German mankind. They saw that not all Germans were these terrible monsters they had to succumb to for the past four years and there was kindness still left in humanity.

Upon arriving in Landsberg, Meier and Naftali explained to the Jewish Organization that they wished to return to their hometown of Kovno, Lithuania. Therefore, Meier and Naftali were placed in trucks that were headed to Munich, Germany. It was explained to them that the people in Landsberg were staying in Landsberg and remaining in the displaced person's camp in an attempt to start their lives over again. In order to return to their country they needed to travel to Munich, Germany and from there they would wait for transport back their country.

According to http://dpcamps.ort.org, "DP Camps (Displaced Persons Camps) started as improvised shelter for about one million five hundred thousand people who were unable to go back after the end of 1945 to the country of their origin. DP camps were primarily organized in Germany, Austria and Italy and located in former military barracks, hospitals, former labor and concentration camps and even partly destroyed structures. The administrations of the camps were initially in the hands of occupying allied military authorities, but later the authority of the camps was transferred to the United Nations Relief and Rehabilitation Administration (UNRAA). By

1952 all but one DP camp was closed. The last DP camp to close was in Germany, Fohrenwald and it closed in 1957.

The DP camp in Landsberg was the second largest camp in the American zone that was located near Munich. Landsberg DP camp was founded in April 1945 after the liberation of Landsberg Concentration Camp. The population in this DP camp had about 5000 Jewish survivors that were Russian, Latvian and Lithuanian descent. The DP camps had many problems such as; lack of food, overcrowding with lack of housing and poor sanitation. Many survivors were waiting to receive help and a place to stay: many slept in attics, basements and garages hoping a praying for a better life. Most of the DP camps were enclosed with barbed wire to keep the victims in; they were only allowed to leave with special passes. They were given black, wet and moldy bread, which barely helped keep the survivors alive. Their meals, once again, just like in the concentration camps consisted of old bread and coffee. The DP camps did not have enough warm clothes for everyone; many had to wear the strip pajamas from the camps for clothes and were freezing during the harsh winters. The places where they were to stay, were unfit for the winter and many died from the cold due to lack of clothing and from starvation. In July 1945, President Truman sent Earl G. Harrison, the dean of the University of Pennsylvania Law School, to investigate the living conditions in these displaced persons camp. He visited over thirty DP camps and stated in his report: "as matters now stand, we appear to be treating the Jews as the Nazis treated them, except that we do not exterminate them."

Despite these issues, the Jews managed to assemble a variety of entertainment activities in certain DP camps for the survivors such as; newspapers, a radio station, a choir, and a theatre which they had shows for everyone to enjoy. Eventually under the administration of the UNRAA some of the DP camps were able to establish a kosher kitchen. The camp also had a major religious life including: a Talmud, Torah, and a Yeshiva place to study. In October 1945, the head of the Zionist Organization in Palestine, David Ben-Gurion, visited the camp.

The Landsberg DP camp also had an educational system from pre-kindergarten to college. This was run by an organization named ORT, which is one of the largest, private, not-for-profit, non-governmental training and education organizations in the world. ORT was founded in St Petersburg in Tsarist, Russia in 1880 to help provide educational and employable skills for the Jewish people. In English, ORT means "The Society for Handicrafts and Agricultural Work".

Landsberg DP camp was the first site for the ORT headquarters and the first training classes began in October 1945. A man by the name of Jacob Oleski started the vocational courses in Landsberg. He was a leader of ORT before the war in Kovno, Lithuania and thanks to him there were vocational training workshops inside the Kovno Ghetto. It was thanks to Jacob Oleski that Naftali was able to stop working in the airfields in Kovno Ghetto and was able to stay inside the ghetto to train in the workshops. By the end of 1947, the school had 300 students who were trained in nursing, garment cutting, tailoring, radio technology, leather work, carpentry, dental technology, auto mechanics and watch repairing to name just a few of the trades. The Landsberg DP camp was closed in October 1950.

Naftali and Meier asked Shmuel and David Koton to join them in their travels back to Kovno, Lithuania but they decided not to return. They chose to remain in Landsberg and start their lives over again in the Displaced Person's camp. David reunited with his wife Shandel who survived Stutthof Concentration Camp and shared with the family what happened to their cousins Hanetkah and Munkha;

who were Uncle Motel's children. Shandel was on the same death march as them and witnessed their execution. It was quite tragic to hear how close they were to freedom and were only days away from liberation. To suffer all those years in the ghetto and then to survive all the brutality and starvation in Stutthof, only to perish on a death march because a Nazi monster decided their lives were not worth living.

Shmuel, David, Shandel and her mother remained in the displaced person's camp in Landsberg for three years. Shandel delivered her first child while still in the camp. After three years, they managed to obtain the paperwork for entry into the United States. All four of them, then packed up what little belongings they had and relocated to New York City to start their lives over, once again.

The trucks going to Munich, Germany were filled with survivors from Dachau Concentration Camp who were from Poland, Hungary,

Czechoslovakia, and Lithuania. Everyone on those trucks had one reason for being on those trucks, to return home in the hope of being reunited with any surviving family members. Look of fear, hope and despair was on everyone's face, for they knew they were probably the only surviving member of their family, but no one was ready to give up hope! One had to believe that someone in their family survived, that the brutal SS Nazis did not manage to exterminate their entire family.

Three days after Meier and Naftali left Landsberg Displaced Person's camp, Hannah and Esther Michelsky arrived; their mother and Naftali's father were brother and sister. Hannah and Esther were both liberated from Bergen Belsen by the British soldiers on April 16, 1945 and were in Poland helping friends with running an orphanage for Jewish children who survived the Holocaust. When they heard of an opportunity to return to Kovno, Lithuania they took a transport to Landsberg, Germany. When arriving in the DP camp, the residents of the camp surrounded their transport. Everyone was there to find a familiar face, to see if any of their family members survived the atrocities. It was there that Hannah and Esther found Shmuel and David Koton alive. Their reunion was bittersweet as they learned about the other family members who did not survive. It was then that Hannah and Esther discovered that their cousins, Naftali and Meier survived and they missed seeing them by 3 days. Hannah and Esther remained in the DP camp in Landsberg; they married there, had their first born in this camp and eventually immigrated to California in the United States.

Upon Naftali's and Meier's arrival to Munich they were assigned to a building. There were many large buildings throughout this DP camp and every building was for a different nationality. There were buildings for Polish survivors, for Hungarian survivors, for Czechoslovakian survivors, for Russian survivors, for Italian survivors, for Lithuanian survivors and many more buildings for all the various nationalities that were persecuted by the Nazis. It appeared there was an endless amount of buildings filled with unfamiliar faces, shallow, pale and gaunt from the evil they had all witnessed and experienced. Everyone there was there for one reason, to find a familiar face, to be reunited with their loved ones, to find a reason why they survived when so many others perished.

Naftali and Meier were waiting for their day to come so they could return to Kovno and hopefully find their mother Rosa, their father Zalman, their sister Zipora, their grandmother Ite Rive, their aunts, their uncles, their cousins and friends. The only family members they knew that survived the war were their Uncle Shmuel Koton, his son David and his wife, Shandel with her mother. Meier wanted to find out if his wife; Bella survived the war as well. It was agony for them to have to wait to return home and then start searching for their family members. Their father was one of seven siblings and their mother was also one of seven siblings and most of them were married. That meant that Meier and Naftali had ten Aunts and ten Uncles, a total of twenty aunts and uncles. Most of their aunts and uncles were married with children and they had a total of nineteen cousins. They prayed that more than Uncle Shmuel and Cousin David survived.

When it was almost Naftali and Meier's turn to board the transports back to Lithuania, they were informed not to go!! A survivor from Lithuania who left several weeks earlier returned to warn all of them that the Russians were capturing the returning survivors and shipping them to labor camps in Siberia. This survivor watched while the Russians were arresting some of the other survivors who returned home to Lithuania. He managed to escape before getting captured and returned to Munich to warn the rest of the survivors not to go back home. It was not safe!!! It was unbelievably disappointing news!

How could they survive the atrocities of the Germans just to now have to suffer the atrocities of the Russians? Was there no end to their pain and suffering? How would they reunite with their family members? How will they discover if any family members survived? Were any of their surviving family members already captured and now serving time in Siberia in their labor camps? So many questions and no way to get any of these questions answered. There was no way now that Meier or Naftali could return to their hometown of Kovno, Lithuania. They were not prepared to confront the Russians and risk being captured and sent to another labor camp. They now had to think quickly as they were expected to leave on the next transport out of the DP camp.

Meier and Naftali snuck out of their building to another building on the other side of the camp to avoid being forced on the transport to Lithuania. There they met a man they recognized from their Ghetto, his name was Bergman. He was in charge of handing out documentations and was put in charge by the American Army. Naftali and Meier were able to finally receive official documentation with their photo; this was their only form of identity; since in the camps they were only a number. Naftali's number was 8176. See photo/documentation at the end of the book.

Chapter Nineteen:

Now that the Americans were taking over this displaced person's camp, they decided to evacuate everyone from this camp and move everyone 50 kilometers away to another displaced person's camp. Meier and Naftali had no interest in moving another 50 kilometers away to another camp. They heard rumors that two times a week, at night, the Jewish Brigade from the British Army would sneak out survivors from the Displaced Person's camp and help them get across the border through Austria to Italy. These British soldiers were Jewish and as a part of the Jewish Brigade, they wanted to help the survivors escape the Displaced Person's camp. At night, twice a week, they would sneak away from their army barracks in covered trucks, then enter the Displaced Person's camp and help any survivor that wanted to leave. They would drive these survivors across the Austrian border and drive through Austria until they approached the mountains that separated

Austria from Italy. These soldiers would then escort the survivors over the mountains into Italy. Once they arrived in Italy, there were other covered trucks waiting for them. The drivers of those trucks were also British soldiers from the Jewish Brigade. Meier and Naftali decided they would sneak out of the camp and head to Italy but in the meantime they needed to find somewhere to stay until the next time the Jewish Brigade would return.

Naftali and Meier heard of Germans living not too far from the Displaced Person's camp that were kind and opening up their homes to survivors. Meier, Naftali and a friend of theirs, Schaget Katz, asked this one German family if they could stay with them for a few nights. Schaget Katz was a friend of Meier and Naftali from their hometown of Kovno. They found him in the displaced person's camp and were all so glad to reunite. At least there were some friends who were still alive!! Unfortunately, he did not know if anyone from his family or Naftali's family survived. He was all alone in the world so Naftali and Meier asked him to join them. At first he shared with them that he was planning on returning to Kovno in an attempt to find any survivors from his family. Meier and Naftali informed him about the Russians capturing survivors and sending them to Siberia, so he then quickly agreed to join them in their escape and travels to Italy. The German family they moved in with were very welcoming and made them all feel very comfortable. While they stayed in this family's home, an older woman, who was a fortuneteller, came over and read Meier's palm. She told Meier that his wife, Bella survived the camps and was alive and well. Meier was so excited and was determined to find her; he vowed he would not stop searching until they were reunited.

Two days later, Meier, Naftali and Schaget Katz left the house to return to the displaced person's camp and wait for the Jewish Brigade to arrive with the covered trucks. This time there were only 15 to 20 survivors on the truck. They left for Austria at night. They had no problems crossing the border into Austria. Once they approached the mountains dividing Austria from Italy, the soldiers helped them off the trucks with their luggage and escorted them across the border into Italy through the mountains. These soldiers brought them to other soldiers also from the Jewish Brigade waiting with their covered trucks. They were then driven to a town in Italy called "Forli". They arrived in the daytime and the houses in this town were beautiful. Italy's 40th Prime Minister, Benito Mussloni, had a country house in this town. Every house had their own courtyard; it looked like paradise.

They were all brought to an empty house in "Forli" where they were able to rest for a few days. After a week, the soldiers from the Jewish Brigade returned to take them all to another village in Italy called "Modena". They all moved into another empty house within the main square but this time the Italian

Police were watching the house. Naftali became very sick with jaundice and they were forced to remain in the house until Naftali recuperated. According to www.nlm.nih.gov "Jaundice is a medical condition with yellowing of the skin or whites of the eyes, arising from excess of the pigment bilirubin. Bilirubin is a yellow chemical in the substance in blood that carries oxygen in your red blood cells. It typically caused by obstruction of the bile duct, by liver disease, or by excessive breakdown of red blood cells." When he finally was better to travel, Meier, Shaget Katz and another survivor by the name of Rufkah Ogali, decided to leave Modena to travel south to Palestine. Unfortunately, the Italian Police would not let them leave. The Jewish Brigade could not help them anymore; they were unable to bring them any further south. They were now on their own to once again escape another restriction in an attempt to travel to Palestine to start their lives over. They were allowed to come and go as they pleased but they were not allowed to leave the house with their luggage. It was unclear as to why they were not allowed to leave but they were held captive once again.

Naftali made friends with another survivor from the house and his name was Rufkah Rogalin. He wanted to join Meier, Naftali and Shaget on their travels to Palestine. He came up with a brilliant idea how to escape the Italian police. Rufkah made friends with an Italian man in the village; this man was very kind and assisted them with their escape. He offered to hold onto their personal belongings until they were able to gather everything to leave the village of Modena. For three days, the men in the house would leave their home wearing two layers of clothing, they would walk over to the Italian man's house and remove the bottom layer of clothing and return to the home to repeat the entire procedure again and again until all their clothes were in the Italian man's house. It took them over three days to bring all their clothes, as they did not want the policemen to be suspicious. When all their clothes and belongings were finally out of the house, Naftali threw their suitcases out the back window for Meier to catch. Unfortunately, the Italian policeman caught Meier with the suitcases. He made Meier open the suitcases and luckily they were all empty. Since the suitcases were empty, the officer allowed Meier to leave with the suitcases. They returned to the Italian's man house to pack up all their clothes and then they left for the train station.

Meier, Naftali, Shaget and Rufkah all left for the train station. When they were on the train, the conductor approached them and asked for their tickets. They told the conductor they had permission and ripped out a page from one of their Jewish books, which the conductor was unable to read or understand therefore, he stamped the paperwork and let them all remain on the train, much to their relief! They traveled south on the train until they reached the village of "Bari" in South Italy.

Chapter Twenty:

Upon arriving to Bari, Italy, Naftali, Meier, Shaget and Rufkah went directly to the where there was a survivor's administration office. This organization was known as UNRRA- United Nations Relief and Rehabilitation Administration. It was founded in June 1943 to provide aid to those people who were liberated from the Germans. As part of its program, UNRRA distributed billions of dollars worth of aid founding shelter, food and rehabilitation programs as well as helping about seven million post-war refugees return to their homes. UNRRA folded its operation in Europe in 1947 and in Asia in 1949. Its functions were transferred to other UN Agencies, including International Refugee Organization (IFO) and United Nations Children's Found (UNICEF).

The men were informed by UNRAA that they were unable to stay in Bari, in the displaced person's camp. It opened in 1946 and had over one thousand five hundred people living inside the camp.

The camp was definitely overcrowded and did not have enough food or living space for those people already inside. Since this camp in Bari, Italy was so close to the port it became a major Displaced Person's Center in South Italy for those people trying to illegally or legally immigrate to Palestine; it was actually called the "Bari Transit Camp".

UNRAA instructed the men to go to "Sannicandro di Bari". There they lived in a house with lots of Romanian Jewish survivors and Polish survivors. The UNRAA provided them all with clothing, water and food. This house was close to the beach so they continued their healing process with days spent at the beach. They met many local Italians who were all very kind. This Italian community was not wealthy but they shared everything with the survivors. Naftali found a job in a kitchen making doughnuts; this allowed him the opportunity to earn some money. During his free time he would play football and volleyball with the locals. They were made to feel comfortable in this small village and they were very welcomed. Naftali, Meier, Shaget and Rufkah stayed in this house for six months.

They learned that a high school was opening up in the town of "Santa Maria" also in Southern Italy. The men all packed up and once again moved into a house with other strangers. This house had one bedroom with four Lithuanian survivors, another bedroom had three Hungarian survivors and one bedroom was a father with his two sons. Everyone there studied Hebrew, Math and History. They studied for six months but unfortunately in 1946 the school was closed down and they were once again forced to relocate.

Meier chose to go to a town named "Fano", Italy but the remainder of the men; Naftali, Shaget and Rufkah went to Rome by train where they went to a little village in the town of Grottaferrata, Italy. It is a small town, located on the lower slopes of the Alban Hills, twenty kilometers south east of Rome. They remained there for one week and then were relocated once again to another small village near Grottaferrata called "Roca di Papa". In 1944, during World War II, this small town was bombed. The Centre of the city was destroyed and thirty-four people perished in that air strike. A second air strike occurred on May 25th 1944 and another thirty-five people died. The American 85th Infantry Division finally liberated the city from the Nazi occupation on June 4, 1944. Naftali, Shaget and Rufkah remained in this small village for four months. They all lived in this house run by UNRAA on top of a mountain with a total of twenty to twenty five survivors. UNRAA continued to supply them with water, food and would occasionally bring them clothing. Naftali was learning how to be a shoemaker and he would repair shoes. After the four months, UNRAA closed the house and everyone needed to relocate once again.

Shaget and Rufkah decided to remain in Rome and Naftali decided to find Meier in Fano, Italy so they all parted ways: wishing everyone safe travels and a better future. A truck came to the house and took all the survivors that wished to travel to Fano. Fano is a town located in the middle of Italy right on the ocean of the Adriatic Sea. It is known for its beaches and is considered a beach resort twelve kilometers (seven miles) southeast of a fishing village called Pesaro, located where the mountain ranges reaches the Adriatic Sea. Fano was also known to be a fishing village and Meier and other survivors were in Fano building fishing boats to go to Palestine. The women in Fano were sewing fishing nets and a Yugoslavian man was teaching everyone to build the boats and sew the nets. They all lived in the fish market; the houses surrounded the center where everyone would come to buy and sell their fish. Naftali remembers building a fishing boat from scratch. They needed to chop down trees for the wood and he worked in a shop to help build the mechanical components for the boat. Naftali remained in Fano for seven months; until the fishing boat was complete.

There existed three types of immigration to Palestine: one legal and two types of illegal immigration. The code name for the legal immigration was known as "Aliyah Alef" where the British allowed survivors to enter Palestine through legal means with proper documentation. The code names for both of the illegal immigrations were known as "Aliyah Bet" and "Aliyah Dalet". "Aliyah Bet" consisted of the secret smuggling of Jews into Palestine without any forged documentation while "Aliyah Dalet" was also illegal but they provided forged documentation to enter Palestine on the pretense of being legal. "Aliyah Dalet" acquired real British passports from the residents in Palestine and then adapted these documents for people in Europe. They tried to match the character traits from the immigrants to match those of the original owners. It was quicker and easier to change an existing document than to produce a new one.   The word "Aliyah" is a Hebrew word (literally, "ascent") and it refers to immigration to the Land of Israel.

There were two phases of "Aliyah Bet". The first, just before and during World War Two was aimed at rescuing European Jews from the Holocaust. Jewish refugees arrived in secret by sea with hundreds of lives lost at sea. Very few Jews managed to escape Europe between 1939 and 1945. Those caught by the British were sent to Mauritius: an island two thousand miles off the southeast coast of Africa. Despite the dangers, sixty-two such voyages were carried out from 1937 to 1944. When the Jewish detainees would arrive in Mauritius, they were imprisoned in a detainment camp in Beau-Bassin; which is a small town in Mauritius. In the camp, the detainees suffered from diseases and inadequate food and clothing. Jewish organizations such as the South African Jewish Board of Deputies, the Jewish Agency, and the Zionist Federation, sent food, clothing, medicine, and religious items to the detainees. The men were held in a former jailhouse and the women were held in nearby iron huts. In total, one hundred and twenty eight prisoners died in the camp, and were buried in the Jewish section of St. Martin Cemetery. At the end of World War II, the detainees were given the choice of returning to their former homes in Europe or immigrating to Palestine. Most chose Palestine, and on August 6, 1945, one thousand three hundred and twenty people landed in Haifa.

The second phase of "Aliyah Bet", took place from the end of the war until the establishment of the State of Israel in 1948. It focused on transporting Jewish survivors into Palestine, especially those housed in Displaced Persons Camps. The passengers were transported on any available boat, which were usually substandard, often old cargo ships, and were overcrowded with passengers. There were one hundred and forty two voyages by one hundred and twenty ships within that time period and over one thousand six hundred survivors drowned at sea. Following the long and uncomfortable journey, over ninety percent of the ships were stopped by the British navy. The Royal British Navy had eight ships on station in Palestine, and additional ships were instructed to track any suspicious vessels heading for Palestine. British authorities forcibly sent the refugees to detention camps, mainly to the Cyprus Internment camps on the Mediterranean island of Cyprus. There were a total of twelve camps in Cyprus, which operated from August 1946 to January 1949. These camps were run by the British government for the imprisonment of the Jewish people who had immigrated or attempted to immigrate to Palestine without proper documentation. Some of the passengers were also sent to the Atlit detention camp in Palestine, and some to Mauritiu. Conditions in the camps were very harsh, with poor sanitation, over-crowding, lack of privacy, and shortage of clean water. The prisoners were mostly young, 80% between thirteen and thirty-five, and included over six thousand orphan children. About two thousand children were born in the camps. Some four hundred Jews died in the camps, and were buried in Margoa cemetery. By 1948 the British held over fifty three thousand five hundred and ten Jewish refugees in internment camps.

From November 1946 to the time of the Israeli Declaration of Independence in May 1948, Cyprus detainees were allowed into Palestine at a rate of seven hundred and fifty people per month. During 1947-1948, special quotas were given to pregnant women, nursing mothers, and the elderly. Released Cyprus detainees amounted to 67% of all immigrants to Palestine during that period. Following Israeli independence, the British began deporting detainees to Israel at a rate of one thousand five hundred per month. They amounted to 40% of all immigration to Israel during the war months of May-September 1948. The British kept about eleven thousand detainees, mainly men of military age, imprisoned throughout most of the war. On January 24, 1949, the British began sending these detainees to Israel, with the last of them departing for Israel on February 11, 1949.

Aliyah Bet transports were organized by the Mossad for Aliyah Bet, which was a part of the Haganah. The Haganah was the secret military branch of the Jewish leadership group, which existed during the British rule over Palestine from 1920 to 1948; it then became the basis for the Israeli defense force. Despite British efforts to curb immigration, during the fourteen years of the Aliyah Bet, over one hundred and ten thousand Jews eventually entered Palestine.

Chapter Twenty-One:

The administration for the Holocaust Survivors that were currently in Fano was responsible for assisting the Mossad in smuggling the Jewish survivors into Palestine ("Aliyah Bet and "Aliyah Dalet"). In 1947, the Jewish Agencies throughout Europe's DP camps who were responsible for selecting survivors to immigrate to Palestine were given specific instructions from David Ben-Gurion: who was the chairman of the World Zionist Organization and the head of the Jewish Agency. He instructed these organizations to issue new documents through "Aliyah Dalet" to mainly young men "fit to fight for their country". The Israelis were preparing for an upcoming war with the Arabs once Israel was declared a country and they needed young, strong soldiers to fight the war of independence.

Initially, the Jewish Agency was carefully selecting immigrants who were suitable for the country's labor and military needs and were single or married men with no children between the ages of 17-25 years old. By the beginning of February 1948, they raised the maximum recruitment age for men to 35 years old. By March 1948, they began recruiting single or married women with no children between the ages of 18 and 25 years old. And on May 4, 1948 all men were recruited between the ages of 17 until 35 but this time they allowed married men with children and men who were in good physical shape, up to the age of 40. Even the immigrants held prisoners in Cyprus were training to be soldiers so when they would be released they would be ready to fight for their country. As per David Ben Gurion "The security issue takes priority even over immigration! Even before the State! Since without an existing military force, there can be no immigration, no state, nothing."

The war depended on immigration because there was not enough manpower in Palestine. The Arabs had enormous manpower and in order to defeat the Arabs to win a victory for the State of Israel all immigration was directed entirely from beginning to end on the needs of the upcoming war. The orders from David Ben Gurion on the selection of immigrants for military recruitment only, were not open for discussion, interpretation or change. The Jewish Agencies throughout Europe's DP camps were to follow the orders exactly. These chosen immigrants traveled to Palestine on ships with false passports provided to them from "Aliyah Dalet". They pretended to be residents of Palestine who were vacationing in Europe but to make the story believable they needed families with children onboard these ships as well. These families with children were needed to balance out the population of "returning residents" so as not to raise the suspicions of the British at the Port. Therefore, some families with children were among the immigrants chosen to set sail across the ocean to Palestine.

In July 1947, the administration chose five men from Fano to travel to Palestine. Naftali was one of the men chosen since he was 20 years old, single with no children and spoke Hebrew. He went to a Hebrew Day School in Kovno before the war and was taught Hebrew. The fact that he spoke Hebrew would make it more believable that he was a resident of Palestine and not trying to smuggle into the country. The country had three spoken languages: Arabic, English and Hebrew. If he spoke Lithuanian when disembarking in Palestine, it would be evident to the British Custom Agents that he was not a resident of Palestine but rather attempting to smuggle into the country and would be sent to Cyprus Detention Camp.

The other four men who were chosen were also between the ages of 17-25, single with no children and were fluent in Hebrew. Meier chose not to go with the men to Palestine as he found out from UNRAA that Bella; his wife had survived the camps and was living in Paris, France with her sister. Bella was in Poland when the Russians liberated Stutthof Concentration Camp on May 9, 1945. Her sister, Tamara, was a Physician in the Russian Army and after the war she left the army to search for her sister. When they reunited, they traveled to Paris, France where they stayed until Meier heard Bella was alive. Meier wrote to Bella through the UNRAA and they arranged to meet.

In the meantime, Naftali and the other four men were preparing for their trip to Palestine. They were sent to Milano, Italy, also known as Milan in English, to train for their departure. Through "Aliyah Dalet" they were given false passports. All the men were provided with passports that claimed they were fishermen. The Mossad for "Aliyah Dalet" took Naftali's photo and attached his photo inside an existing passport therefore giving him a new identification. Naftali's name was now Pinchus Kravitz. He was a fisherman who lived in Palestine.

They were all taught how to act like an Israeli. They were taught the layout of the port in Haifa, so when they got off the ship, they would walk with confidence and not act like they were lost or unfamiliar with the port. They taught them where all the surrounding buildings in the port were located, even where the bathrooms could be found and instructed them how to walk with authority and where the bus stop would be. They were instructed on the currency in Palestine and to have the correct change for the bus. They taught them to act aggressively when boarding the bus: to push themselves onto the bus even if there was no room. This was how the Israelis and Arabs acted and if they appeared uncomfortable in this surrounding or too accommodating to others then the British police would arrest them. The British police patrolled Haifa port and watched everyone for any suspicious behavior. The Mossad for "Aliyah Dalet" was not interested in spending hours of manpower preparing these men to travel and immigrate to

Palestine and provide them with documentation just for them to get arrested upon arriving to Palestine.

Chapter Twenty Two:

After their two-week training session in Milano, Italy, the five men were moved to Torino, Italy also known as Turin in English. There they were expected to pack up packages of food for their own Aliyah and as well for the other immigrants traveling through "Aliyah Bet". The American Army was supplying the British Army with food packages. There were Jewish soldiers who were a part of the British Army and they were supporting the illegal immigration of survivors to Palestine. They would smuggle out food packages from their barracks and bring them to the Mossad who were responsible for the illegal immigration to Palestine. The Mossad would also receive parcels of food from UNRAA as well. The immigrants would then assemble these packages to take on their journey and for others to take on their journey across the ocean to Palestine.

After another two weeks in Torino, Italy, the men were moved one last time and this time it was to

Genoa, Italy. Genoa is also known as Genova in Italian. It is one of Europe's largest cities on the Mediterranean Sea and it has the largest seaport in Italy. The port of Genoa was the main transit center for Jewish emigrants who came primarily from Eastern Europe and were heading for Palestine, either legally or illegally.

Naftali and the other four men he was training with from Fano, Italy all boarded the ship to Italy on October 9, 1947. The ship was filled with legal British citizens who were on vacation in Italy but they all lived in Palestine. The five men shared a cabin and their journey to Palestine was uneventful. They ate their meals in a dining hall with other passengers and pretended to be the individuals in their passports: fishermen from Palestine on vacation in Italy. They never shared with anyone on the ship that they were illegal immigrants trying to smuggle into Palestine. One was never too certain who would hear and tell the British upon arriving into Palestine.

When Naftali docked in Palestine, he was met by border agents. His agent was an Arab policeman who asked to see Naftali's Passport. According to the information in the Passport, Pinchus Kravitz was born in Alexandra, Egypt but his family relocated to Jerusalem when he was two years old. This explained why Pinchus did not speak Arabic but rather he did speak Hebrew. It was not a law that you needed to speak Arabic so there were no problems with Naftali's passport and he answered all the questions appropriately and therefore was allowed to enter Palestine!! What a relief!! What an exciting time!!

Naftali knew he still had to be careful because throughout the Port were British police and they were watching everyone closely for any suspicious behavior. He was not in the free and clear yet. Naftali and the four other men from Fano all walked towards the bus station with confidence as it was located exactly where it was described to them.

They boarded the bus like locals and had the correct currency and exact change. No one gave them a second look as they blended in perfectly. They were all trained very well for this illegal immigration and all five of them successfully immigrated to Palestine.

They were instructed as to which stop to exit and from there they met up with a man who worked for "Aliyah Dalet". They were all brought to a hotel, where they stayed for two nights. On the third day, another man from "Aliyah Dalet" arrived and provided them all with documentation which had their real names, the date they arrived in the port of Haifa and placed a new photo in this documentation. They took back their passports, as it was necessary for "Aliyah Dalet" to reuse the passports to help smuggle more survivors from Italy into Palestine.

While the men sat in their hotel room waiting for their new documentation, they witnessed the British Army erecting a two-story fence outside their hotel, as the British Police station was located there. They found out this was for the British Army's protection. Two weeks before their arrival, the Jewish underground rolled a barrel with explosives into the British Police station and killed many British Police Officers. The British officers were not willing to take any further chances of attacks so they built this fence to keep everyone out and them inside for protection.

During the Second World War, the Intelligence agencies of Britain and the Jewish Agency for Palestine had often worked together to fight Nazi, Germany. The Jewish Agency cooperated with Britain, in the hopes that after the war, the British would lift the sanctions on the number of Jewish immigrants allowed to enter Palestine. By 1945, when it became clear that Britain was not fulfilling the expectations to lift immigration restrictions on Jews to Palestine, David Ben-Gurion, launched a secret war against the British police and their British policies. This explained why the British police were erecting a two-story fence around their station. They feared for their safety with the Jewish underground around.

After providing the five men with their official landing papers, they drove them to a Kibbutz about 25 kilometers from Tel-Aviv, called Kibbutz Tel Yitzhak. Tel Yitzhak is located in central Israel, in the coastal plain to the southeast of a town called Netanya. According to the www.urbandictionary.com "A kibbutz is an Israeli concept of a farm-residence. The basic principle is that anyone can come in, stay and be fed, as long as they work towards the upkeep of the kibbutz. One can stay for two days or for a lifetime. There are 278 kibbutzim (plural of kibbutz) in Israel. They are often strictly Orthodox Jewish - requiring no work to be done on the Sabbath, which starts on Friday night and ends on Saturday night. They are the basic Communist template, because often no money is exchanged in the residence/farming transactions."

When Naftali and the other four men arrived to Kibbutz Tel Yitzhak, they were given one week vacation to rest and tour Israel. They moved into tents, two men to one tent and inside there were two beds and one table. Life was not easy in the kibbutz and there were no luxuries but no one complained because they were free.

Chapter Twenty-Three:

Naftali decided he wanted to tour Palestine and his first stop would be Jerusalem. He became friendly with a fellow kibbutznik (another member of the kibbutz) and they traveled together to Kibbutz Ramat Rachel. Ramat Rachel is a kibbutz located on top of hill overlooking the magnificent panorama of Jerusalem's Old City, the Dead Sea, and the Judean Hills. This kibbutz was established in 1926. He dropped Naftali off and left to go pick up his girlfriend. He told Naftali to meet him outside the Kibbutz at 4:00pm and they would travel together to Jerusalem.

While Naftali was waiting for his friend to come pick him up, he saw a taxi and waved it down, thinking his friend was inside. He was completely wrong and out from the taxi jumped four soldiers, two British and two Arabs. They immediately began questioning Naftali and asked to see his papers. Thankfully he had the documentation that "Aliyah

Dalet" provided him and they reviewed his papers carefully. They then began to search him; they discovered a pen and took it apart searching for anything suspicious. They detained Naftali for over half an hour and it was quite frightening. He had no idea what they were looking for or what they would do with him or to him. They finally allowed Naftali to leave with his documentation and his pen. Later on, Naftali learned that the Jewish Underground were using pens for guns and were shooting make shift bullets from these pens. That did help explain why they searched Naftali's pen so thoroughly.

Eventually, Naftali's friend and his friend's girlfriend did arrive to Kibbutz Ramat Rachel and they traveled together to tour Jerusalem. Naftali was surprised to see that Jerusalem was primarily filled with Arabs and very few Jewish residents. It was a bit shocking for Naftali as this was not the Jerusalem he envisioned all his years. Jerusalem was totally isolated from other Jewish settlements in the country, surrounded by numerous Arab villages and subject to British rule which tended to side with the Arabs.

When they returned to the kibbutz, their vacation was over and they were assigned a job to protect the kibbutz by sitting in the observation tower and patrolling the perimeter of the kibbutz for the British Army. Each kibbutz had their specific instructions from David Ben Gurion on how to assist the Jewish underground with their fight against the British authority. The members of Kibbutz Tel Yitzhak were developing explosive powder. They would roll the powder out on a screen and it would come out like strands of spaghetti, they would then place these strands of explosives in the oven to dry them out and then it would be ready to be used for gunpowder. This was all illegal work and therefore they needed to keep a watch for the British Army, who would randomly come into the Kibbutz to search for illegal arms or any illegal activity. When the men on patrol would see the British Army approaching the Kibbutz, they would release the chickens from the chicken coops. This would cause a huge commotion as it was difficult for the soldiers to walk inside the Kibbutz to investigate and it would give the Kibbutzniks time to clean up the gunpowder, its residue and hide all the equipment. The members of the kibbutz would rotate patrolling the kibbutz every month and they would patrol for an entire week. This way everybody assisted with the security of the Kibbutz.

There was another kibbutz not too far away that made illegal bullets; it was called the "Ayalon Institute". In fact, it was not really a kibbutz but rather a secret ammunition factory set up by the Jewish underground. The members of that "kibbutz" built a factory in less than one month's time, 13 feet underground with nearly 2-foot-thick walls and ceiling. The only way to access this underground factory was either by moving the large washing machine in the laundry room or by moving the 10-ton oven in the bakery, which one could move along a set of metal runners. These machines camouflaged the noise of manufacturing bullets. To conceal the sound of the machinery in the factory, the laundry was kept running 24 hours a day.

This kibbutz was located directly in front of a British Army Base. The kibbutz offered to wash the uniforms for the British Army and since they did such a good job cleaning clothes, the British officials agreed to bring their uniforms to be laundered at the kibbutz. To keep the soldiers away, the kibbutz members provided a pick up and delivery service to their enemies.

One of the components needed for the factory was copper to make the bullet casings. To conceal the purpose of the purchases, the Jews applied to import copper for what they said were cases for kosher lipstick. The British accepted this explanation, which was reinforced by gifts from the Jews of lipstick cases to the British officials. Once the bullets were finished they would put them inside milk canisters and smuggle them out from the factory in the tunnel that was underneath the oven in the bakery. These canisters would then be removed and loaded onto trucks, but these canisters were much too heavy. Later, secret compartments were built inside fuel trucks to hide the bullets. Since the British didn't expect anything as explosive as bullets to be hidden in fuel trucks, the Jews were able to distribute the bullets around the country without detection. In its two years of production this factory manufactured over 2,500,000 9mm bullets that were used in Sten guns.

The Jewish Underground was very clever and they helped this kibbutz by blowing up a bridge directly outside the "Ayalon Institute", while a trainload of British soldiers were on the train. After the explosion, members from the "Ayalon Institute" ran out to the site of the accident with stretchers to help save the British soldiers. They brought them back to the kibbutz and administered first aid to the soldiers. The British Army was so appreciative for the help they received from this kibbutz that they seldom came inside the kibbutz to inspect. They trusted them and felt that out of respect they should leave them alone. This allowed the factory to work day and night manufacturing the bullets without any delays from the British Army.

Naftali's kibbutz, Kibbutz Tel Yitzhak, was also quite busy producing their own food. They had a huge banana farm where they grew bananas, they also had a large vegetable garden with carrots, cucumbers and peppers as well an orchard with grapes and apples, they had chickens to lay eggs and cows to produce milk and corn was growing in their corn fields. The kibbutz would sell their grapes and carrots to help support the kibbutz and their illegal activity. Naftali was assigned to work as a plumber in the fields making and repairing the sprinklers for the fruit and vegetable gardens. He enjoyed being outdoors and was able to eat the fruit and vegetables while he worked. He was still very skinny from his years in the ghetto and the concentration camps so the other men told him to eat lots of bananas to fatten himself up. Naftali remembers eating 28 bananas, he developed such terrible stomach pains; he never ate bananas again!

By the end of 1947, the Jewish underground was now fighting the Arabs as well as the British Army. The Arabs started shooting into the kibbutzim while the people were trying to collect their harvest. Since the Arabs were attacking all the kibbutzim, the members of the kibbutz needed to protect themselves. Naftali remembers having to go out with rifles to guard and protect the people while they were collecting the corn. One night, in the middle of the night, Naftali was awoken from his sleep and instructed to go into the lunchroom. In the lunchroom were ten other men from his kibbutz. They were all handed rifles and instructed to board a truck waiting for them outside the Kibbutz. This truck was driving them to Tel-Monde where they were going to meet other kibbutzniks in order to attack an Arab village. This was the Arab village that continuously kept attacking the kibbutzim in the area and they had enough. They thought if they scared them they would stop!

When they arrived to Tel-Monde there were over 120 men there from kibbutzim throughout the area. They all walked into a small forest/wheat field across the Arab village to prepare for their attack and wait for their instructions. Naftali remembers it was terribly hot and uncomfortable standing there waiting for their instructions. Their commander ordered for all of them to enter the Arab village but unfortunately the Arabs were expecting them. They brought reinforcements from other Arab villages and the Kibbutzniks were ambushed. The Arabs opened fire on the Kibbutzniks and everybody was running in every different direction. Naftali was able to get a stretcher and he was trying to help a fellow kibbutznik who was shot and injured. He ran in a zig-zag out from the fields to avoid being hit by bullets, to safety. Twenty-eight men died that night and two of them were friends of his from his kibbutz. It was such a tragic night and they lost their lives for nothing!!!

In November 1947, the United Nations voted to separate Palestine into two countries (one Jewish, one Arab). British troops began to withdraw from Palestine in April 1948, and in May 1948 the Zionist leader David Ben-Gurion proclaimed the establishment of the modern state of Israel. All limitations on Jewish immigration were immediately lifted, finally.

Chapter Twenty Four:

Today, Naftali Schlomowitz lives in Montreal, Canada. He has a wife named Nechama Schlomowitz. They met on a blind date in Israel and they will be celebrating their 58th wedding anniversary on July 25th, 2014. They have two daughters, Varda van Osnabrugge and Jennie Schneider. Varda was born in Israel and Jennie was born in Montreal, Quebec, Canada. Naftali and Nechama moved to Canada in the summer of 1963 to reunite with Meier and Bella. Varda's husband is Jan and they have two sons named Sean and Aron. They all live in Toronto, Canada. Jennie's husband is Jack and they have three daughters -including me- named Samantha, Nicole (me), and Sydney. We all live in Lake Worth, Florida.

Naftali is currently approaching his 87th birthday on February 16th, 2014. Naftali and Nechama's grandchildren call them both Grampi and Granny. They are snowbirds, so they come down to

Florida for six months of the year to spend time with their granddaughters: Samantha, Nicole, and Sydney.

My grandfather is my hero. He is always there for me and I love him so much. Every time he tells me a new story about his life, I enjoy learning new details about him. His life is so interesting; he is a walking history book. Spending quality time with my Grampi is what I look forward to, especially playing card games together such as touch and rummi-500. Three words I would use to describe him are: brave, ingenious and strong. He has survived so much and I am so proud that I can call him my grandfather. I love him so much and cannot wait to spend more time with him every year he comes to visit.

Naftali's Father's Family Tree

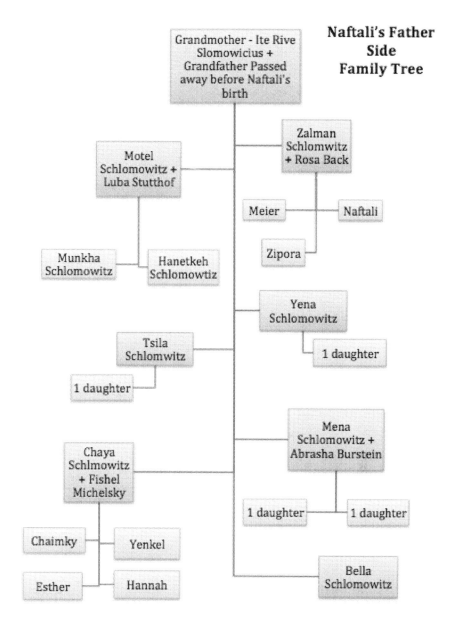

Naftali's Father Side Family Tree

Grandmother - Ite Rive Slomowicius + Grandfather Passed away before Naftali's birth

Zalman Schlomwitz + Rosa Back

Motel Schlomowitz + Luba Stutthof

Meier — Naftali

Zipora

Munkha Schlomowitz

Hanetkeh Schlomowtiz

Yena Schlomowitz

1 daughter

Tsila Schlomwitz

1 daughter

Mena Schlomowitz + Abrasha Burstein

Chaya Schlmowitz + Fishel Michelsky

1 daughter — 1 daughter

Chaimky — Yenkel

Esther — Hannah

Bella Schlomowitz

Naftali's Mother's Family Tree

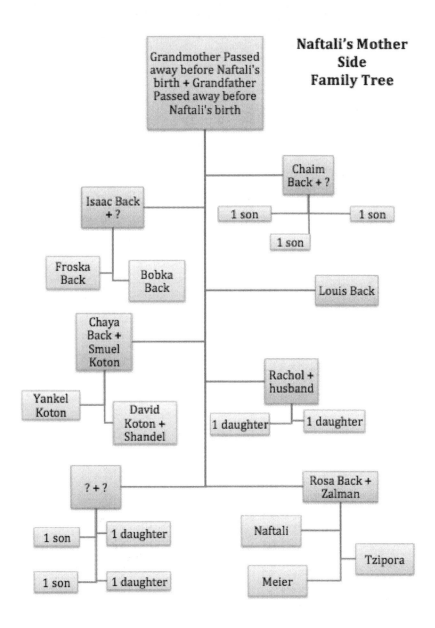

Naftali's Mother
Side
Family Tree

Grandmother Passed away before Naftali's birth + Grandfather Passed away before Naftali's birth

Chaim Back + ?

Isaac Back + ?

1 son

1 son

1 son

Froska Back

Bobka Back

Louis Back

Chaya Back + Smuel Koton

Rachol + husband

Yankel Koton

David Koton + Shandel

1 daughter

1 daughter

? + ?

Rosa Back + Zalman

1 son

1 daughter

Naftali

1 son

1 daughter

Meier

Tzipora

Photos

Family photo before the war.

The story is in chapter three. This picture is from the book *Hidden History of the Kovno Ghetto*.

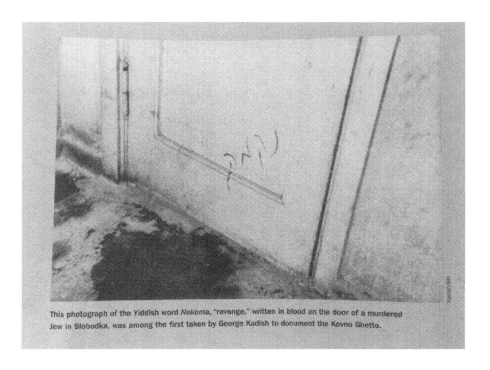

This photograph of the Yiddish word *Nekoma*, "revenge," written in blood on the door of a murdered Jew in Slobodka, was among the first taken by George Kadish to document the Kovno Ghetto.

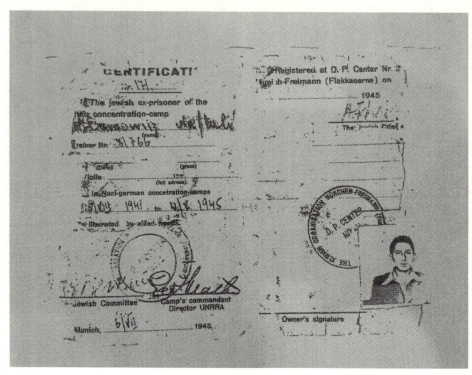

Naftali's documentation from imprisonment at Dachau Concentration Camp.

Naftali's immediate family: (top to bottom) Zalman Schlomowitz (Father), Meier Schlomowitz (Older Brother), Rosa Schlomowitz (Mother), Naftali Schlomowitz, and Tzipora Schlomowitz (Younger Sister). This was the picture that Naftali kept in his shoe while in Dachau Concentration Camp.

From left to right: Nechama Schlomowitz (Grandmother), Naftali Schlomowitz (Grandfather), Samantha Schneider (Older Sister), Jack Schneider (Father), Nicole Schneider (Me), Jennie Schneider (Mother), Sydney Schneider (Younger Sister), Varda van Osnabrugge (Aunt), Abe Donagi (Cousin).

Nicole Schneider (me) on the left
My grandfather, Grampi (Naftali Schlomowitz) on the right.

Acknowledgements

Thank you so much Grampi for letting me interview you and sharing your history with me. I know how hard it must have been to share your story with me, as my mother told me that while growing up, you would never discuss the details of your years in the Holocaust with anyone. I promise you that what you shared with me will never be forgotten and what you suffered will not be in vain. You survived your ordeal and finally shared your story so that history should never repeat itself. You witnessed mankind at his worst and persevered to fight the war of independence in Israel, marry and raise a beautiful family of your own. Your story shook me to my core realizing how lucky I am to have you here, sitting beside me and everything you went through to survive. As hard as it was to hear everything you endured, you are an incredible part of history and now with this book your suffering and struggles to survive will be remembered forever.

Thank you mom for reading over my work and helping me interpret Grampi's story. Thank you Granny B. for giving me the idea to write my book on Grampi's holocaust story. Thank you Mrs. Jurskis for always saying I could complete the book, for all the encouragement, and the helpful critique. Thank you to all of my family for their support. I could not have done it without you guys.

Bibliography:

Bülow, Louis. "Gates to Hell." *The Holocaust-The Nazi Genocide.* N.p., n.d. Web. <http://www.deathcamps.info>.

Dann, Sam. *Dachau 29 April 1945: The Rainbow Liberation Memoirs.* Lubbock, TX: Texas Tech UP, 1998. Print.

"Definition of Death Marches." *Definition of Death Marches.* N.p., n.d. Web. 25 Nov. 2013. <http://fcit.usf.edu/HOLOCAUST/DEFN/deathma.HTM>.

Distel, Barbara, and Ruth Jakusch. *Concentration Camp Dachau, 1933-1945.* Brussels: Comité International De Dachau, 1978. Print.

"The Gay Lovers Quarrel That Ignited the Nazi Atrocity Kristallnacht." *Frank Sanello's History as Front Page News.* N.p., n.d. Web. <http://www.historyasfrontpagenews.com/>.

Hidden History of the Kovno Ghetto. N.p.: United States Holocaust Memorial Museum, 1997. Print.

"The Holocaust, Ghetto, Kristallnacht, Kovno Ghetto, Lithuania, Final Solution, Death March, Book

Burning." *United States Holocaust Memorial Museum*.
United States Holocaust Memorial Museum, n.d. Web.
<http://www.ushmm.org>.

Lind, Mr. "The German Master Race." *Pure Aryan
Germans.*   N.p.,   n.d.   Web.
<http://www.schoolhistory.co.uk/>.

Lisciotto,   Carmelo.   "The   Kovno   Ghetto
Www.HolocaustResearchProject.org." *The   Kovno
Ghetto Www.HolocaustResearchProject.org*. N.p., n.d.
Web.   25   Nov.   2013.
<http://www.holocaustresearchproject.org/ghettos/
kovno.html>

Mishell, William W. *Kaddish for Kovno: Life and Death
in a Lithuanian Ghetto, 1941-1945*. Chicago, IL:
Chicago Review, 1988. Print.

Tory, Avraham, Martin Gilbert, and Dina Porat.
Surviving the Holocaust: The Kovno Ghetto Diary.
Cambridge, MA: Harvard UP, 1990. Print.

39416858R00126

Made in the USA
Lexington, KY
22 February 2015